SCORECARD MARKETING

The four-step playbook for getting
better leads and bigger profits

DANIEL PRIESTLEY
WITH GLEN CARLSON

Re^think

First published in Great Britain in 2022
by Rethink Press (www.rethinkpress.com)

Cover image © Richard Burch

Illustrations by Andrew Priestley

*We dedicate this book to entrepreneurs
all over the world who are using their
businesses to solve meaningful problems.
We hope this helps you to stand out and
scale up in these remarkable times.*

CONTENTS

INTRODUCTION

Everything in business is downstream from lead generation. If you can't capture the attention of customers, investors, partnerships and potential talent and generate a signal of interest, then it doesn't matter how great your offer is. If the leads dry up, the sales stop flowing and the best salespeople leave. Then the revenue starts dropping and the investors want out. Growth stops, the fun stops and the business comes crashing down.

To bring in a customer, first you will need leads – a list of people who might buy. If you want a great employee, you'll need warm leads in the form of people who might be suitable for your team. If you want an investor, your warm leads will be those who might invest in your business. Generating leads is the first step towards finding the right customer, partner, employee or investor.

A warm lead is someone who has given you a signal of interest, such as filling in a form, booking a ticket to an event or requesting more information. As they hand over their contact details to a business, they demonstrate their willingness to engage further, to learn more and to potentially buy.

People are not silly. They know that when they give their information to a business they might as well be putting their hand up in the air, waving and saying, 'I'm interested!' They know there will likely be a sales call or some marketing material to follow.

Getting people to take this first step is an art form. You have to find them and get their attention; you must educate or entertain them and then you have to get them to want to signal their interest. In a perfect scenario you will gain more than basic information about them too – you want valuable insights that will allow you to create a powerful sales and marketing follow-up process.

A flow of warm leads, especially with useful additional data, quickly turn into sales. Sales generate revenue. Revenue proves to investors your business has a future. Investment powers a growing team of passionate people who have fun bringing out the best in each other. Passionate A-players grow the business and make it profitable.

Success and failure look pretty grand from a distance but up close what you are seeing is the compounding effect of a lot of things happening after those first leads came in.

MY FIRST SUCCESSFUL CAMPAIGNS

When I was nineteen I had the opportunity to work with an amazing mentor who taught me all about business while we launched and built an AU$6 million revenue company in two years. Most of those key lessons related directly to lead generation.

The business launched with a successful direct mail campaign. The letter we sent out to over 15,000 people persuaded more than 300 people to show up to a launch event. That event brought in over AU$180K of sales. We then used that money to take out ads in a newspaper and more leads came in. We ran more events and we made more sales.

We repeated this formula week in week out, and within twenty-four months the business had grown from four people around a kitchen table to sixty people in an inner-city Melbourne office.

I left that business at twenty-one to launch my first start-up with Glen Carlson. Our first move was to run ads in the newspaper and generate leads. I remember that on the first day I ran an AU$7,000 quarter-page ad paid for on my credit card. Only a dozen leads came in and I was devastated – I thought our business was over before it had begun.

The following day the phones started ringing. Another seventy people called that week and from those leads Glen and I made AU$31,500 in sales. We ran the ads again; we generated more warm leads and made more sales.

At the end of the first year, we had become a well-oiled lead generation and sales machine. We generated 100+ warm leads per week, we warmed people up to doing business with us with a weekly workshop and we made consistent sales – over AU$1.3 million with a profit of almost AU$400K.

The success didn't stop. Once we had figured out how to generate warm leads, we discovered how valuable this skill was. For a success fee, I consulted for two businesses on their lead generation strategy and earned over AU$90,000 for a few days' 'work'. Then we struck a deal to partner with a start-up business to scale them up and in one year we grew the operation from AU$1 million to AU$10 million.

How did this business grow by ten times in one year? Nothing changed about the underlying business, we simply flooded them with warm leads.

In my twenties and thirties I worked with several millionaires and billionaires and each time I saw the obsession with lead generation. 'Attention is the most valuable currency in business – no attention no business,' was a lesson I learned from a successful entrepreneur.

Why is attention valuable? Because if a lot of people are paying attention, many of them will likely show interest in buying something. That signal of interest is a lead – that lead starts the domino effect that catalyses the success you want from the business.

MANUFACTURING DEMAND

If you have leads flowing in, you can solve almost any other problem. When I have raised investment, investors always ask: 'How will you generate leads and make sales?' Investors will give you money to solve any other problem if you can demonstrate an influx of leads. Talented people will quit their job and come work with you if you have an influx of leads. You can also sell any business with plenty of leads coming in.

Conversely, if you have developed a great product but no one seems interested in buying it, investors and talented people will rarely engage. I have seen hundreds of entrepreneurs who have a great service to offer the world but don't know how to generate warm leads.

In the industrial age, it was difficult to manufacture a product but it was relatively easy to sell it. Something as simple as a pair of scissors required a hundred workers, a plant and equipment to produce at scale but, once they were made, people flocked to buy them. The hard part was keeping up with the orders.

We get the term 'gross domestic product' from this era, when people measured the economy based on how much could be produced. The default assumption was that if it could be made, it could be sold. Fortunes were made by people who could create things.

That isn't true today. It's become easy to make things and consumers are drowning in choices. An Amazon search for 'scissors' brings up pages upon pages of options. You can buy giant novelty scissors or tiny little scissors that fit in a purse. There are dozens of different types of hair scissors, office scissors, kitchen scissors, craft scissors, medical-kit scissors or gardening scissors – and that's before you've even thought about choosing from all the colours available.

In the industrial age, if you could manufacture scissors you would have a huge demand for them. Today, consumers are spoilt for choice and the difficult part is getting them to choose your product over hundreds of alternatives.

An entrepreneur's job today is not about the means of production, it's about the means of distribution. The fortune doesn't go to the person who can make something, it goes to the person who can sell it.

You are still in a manufacturing business but now you must manufacture the demand. You must create a predictable assembly line that produces interested people who are excited to engage with your business.

QUALITY LEAD GENERATION AT SCALE

In this book we simplify the steps to getting warm leads. By the time you finish reading, you will have a clear strategy for something that most people struggle with. Not only will you have set up a remarkable lead generation asset for your business, but you will also have signalled you're interested in doing business with us too.

How can we be so sure? In 2016 we discovered a powerful tool for generating warm leads – a **scorecard**.

We launched the Key Person of Influence Scorecard so that people could benchmark their ability to influence. The website has an attractive **landing page** that clearly describes why someone would want to become a Key Person of Influence and what they should measure if they wanted to improve.

It invites people to complete a **short questionnaire** consisting of forty yes/no questions. After answering these questions, the person receives a **full report** on their strengths and weaknesses, with customised recommendations on how to improve. They can see the report immediately on the screen and receive an extended version via email.

People loved it and continue to love it – over 15,000 people per year complete this scorecard. Our salespeople can't believe their luck.

The sales team can see the results of the questionnaire, which enables them to have a sensible and powerful conversation with each person. Prior to this innovation, we ran events and workshops to generate leads. These workshops were expensive, stressful and labour intensive to run. They were helpful in warming people up to doing business with us, but they had a significant problem: we knew next to nothing about the people who came to our workshops until we spoke to them one-to-one.

It was typical to start a sales call with 'tell me a bit about yourself' and have absolutely no idea what the client would say. We didn't know if they were the CEO of a NASDAQ-listed unicorn or the owner of a fish and chip shop down the road.

The scorecard changed everything.

Scorecards are infinitely scalable at a low cost, and by collecting buckets of data about every person, scorecards give your potential client instant gratification and a person-alised experience.

91% of consumers say they will more likely purchase from brands that provide offers and recommendations relevant to them.[1]

On Spotify, Facebook, Netflix, YouTube and Amazon we're surrounded by extreme personalisation every day, and con-sumers have come to expect that same level of relevance from companies of all sizes. Investing in personalisation to build relationships and create better experiences can pay off with serious rewards for brands. In a world where the vast majority of companies are focused on improving personalisation, com-panies that don't prioritise creating a tailored experience run the risk of getting left behind.

Scorecards are fast, fun and full of relevant information. It's a win-win.

HOW TO USE THIS BOOK

Practical and focused on one clear strategy, this book is not 101 Ways to Generate Leads – you can google those kinds of lists. This is a playbook for successfully implementing a scorecard marketing campaign.

Part One: The Philosophy Of Generating Warm Leads offers a range of marketing philosophies and examples to help you understand the importance of generating warm leads so you can benefit from everything that comes downstream from there.

Part Two: Setting Up A Scorecard walks you through the four-step process of setting up a successful scorecard for your business so you have a marketing machine that delivers more warm leads every week. We also share some case studies from those who have already implemented the strategy in their businesses.

Throughout the book you will find 'action steps' – questions designed for you to answer to gather useful information for later. There are also research statistics that demonstrate key points of the scorecard strategy, and at the end of the book you will find links to many of the resources and tools we mention in our discussions.

If your business could benefit from getting to know people better, scorecard marketing will be invaluable for you. If better qualified leads would result in bigger profits and more fun, this book will give you what you're looking for.

SCOREAPP SOFTWARE MAKES THIS STRATEGY EASY

This scorecard marketing strategy became so important to us that we studied it in detail and refined it endlessly. We then created the software platform ScoreApp.com to encompass everything you need to make this strategy work for your business quickly, efficiently and cost-effectively.

ScoreApp can be your main tool for generating warm leads every month. You could cobble together some Google forms or hire developers and build your own scorecards (that's what we did to start with too) but we think you'll prefer having our team of fanatics building the best system for you.

You have a free trial of our software with this book to see if it works for you as well as it has for thousands of our happy clients, so here is the link for an extended free trial of ScoreApp. There are no commitments – you can cancel at any time.

🔗 **www.scoreapp.com/book-trial**

PART ONE

THE PHILOSOPHY OF GENERATING WARM LEADS

WHY PEOPLE BUY

This book is about you achieving better marketing and sales results. We assume you have something great to sell and want to sell more of it to the right people – to do this, you need a powerful strategy for generating warm leads that convert into paying clients.

The logical place to start is in the mind of someone who might buy from you. We need to explore why they buy, how they build enough trust to signal their interest and the conditions that need to be right for a sale to be made.

PSYCHOLOGICAL TENSION

The underlying reason people buy anything is due to *psychological tension*. People feel a tension between what they have and what they want. They are living in their current reality but they have a desired reality in mind that they believe would be better.

A person who pays for a business coach does so because they feel a psychological tension between the business they have and the business they imagine having in the future. They might have a business that is good by many people's standards but they feel chained to it. Perhaps they feel that it's too much hard work and they have to make every sale. One day they meet up with some parents at the school gate who have just been on a long international holiday with their family. The dissatisfaction builds into a psychological tension, which drives them to be on the lookout for something that might resolve it.

Every customer who has ever bought from your business did so to relieve a psychological tension they were experiencing. They imagined that life would be better after buying what you were offering.

I'm sure you recognised this in some of your customers but there will have been many cases when you didn't – customers who didn't tell you much about themselves and played down their reasons for buying from you. They probably talked about the features of your product or focused on things like the price or the payment terms. They may have concealed their underlying psychological tension but you can be certain it was there. Understanding this tension in your potential customers is important if you want to be successful in your business and make more sales.

Businesses that are clear about the tensions they resolve create better marketing materials, charge better prices, have more powerful sales meetings and deliver better products and services.

Many strong emotions are driven by an underlying tension. Pain, disappointment or dissatisfaction are all forms of tension based on something you have that you wish would stop or change. Desire, lust or longing are different types of tension based on something you don't have but want. Feelings of frustration, annoyance or anger arise from tension based on something not working the way you imagine it should.

Imagine being able to look at a potential customer and see a dashboard glowing above their head telling you exactly what their tension is. Imagine an accountant talking to a business owner and above their head it says, 'I rate myself three out of ten for business finances – this is caused by my cashflow worries.' It would be easy for this accountant to talk to the client about ways to continue working in the business while outsourcing their finances to the accounting firm.

84% of consumers say being treated like a person, not a number, is important to winning their business.[2]

Imagine what it would be like for you and your sales team to have access to this dashboard for every potential client you talk to. This data would speed up every sale, and would lead to more effective marketing campaigns and happier customers.

It would also allow you to raise your prices and measure the impact of your product.

Scorecard marketing enables you to generate warm leads that come in with this data attached. Rather than just seeing people at a surface level, you will know what's driving them and have access to data that reveals exactly why they want to buy something. You will clearly see the tension they are experiencing and be able to quantify it with numbers and zoom in on specific issues that they want to address.

ACTION STEP

Complete the Sales and Marketing Excellence Scorecard to have experience of what it's like to complete a scorecard yourself:

   🔗 **https://laps.scoreapp.com**

AWAKEN DORMANT DESIRES

Sometimes people experience psychological tension that sits deep beneath the surface. They bury it and don't do anything about it, distracting themselves with other things. We call this a dormant tension – a desire or frustration that is not being acted on.

This could be for several reasons. They might have tried to do something about it in the past and it didn't work. It might not be as painful or urgent as other things in their life. They might imagine that there's too much work or expense required to fix a problem they have or that the reward isn't worth it. Maybe they don't believe they're capable of doing something they wish they could do.

Imagine Kelly, a busy mother who used to love going to yoga classes before having kids. Yoga used to be Kelly's reset and it was great for fitness and meeting like-minded friends. Since having young kids, yoga has taken a backseat and now those needs are no longer being fulfilled. This manifests itself in many ways: a lack of energy, feeling unfit and disconnected from a vibrant social circle.

Kelly is probably not looking into yoga classes, though. She knows there is a yoga studio seven minutes down the road but she's buried her desire. The yoga studio doesn't even know Kelly exists or that she might want to get back into her practice.

Imagine if somehow the yoga studio could interview Kelly and ask her what's stopping her from returning. Her response might be that her evenings are taken up with family activities and that she doesn't feel like being around a social circle of people who are single and childless anymore. She might also say that she misses the feeling yoga brings and the added energy it gives her.

What Kelly doesn't know is that the yoga studio has classes for parents with children. These classes are at a time that works, the social circle is perfect and the energy uplift is just as good. If the yoga studio knew why Kelly wasn't coming to classes, they could give her the relevant information; if Kelly had that relevant information, she would absolutely love to come back to yoga classes.

A dormant tension sits beneath the surface waiting to bubble up. The exciting thing is that most people have dormant psychological tensions sitting beneath the surface. For every person who is actively looking for a product or service, there are hundreds of others who might be interested but aren't looking.

If you went to a football match and asked the whole stadium, 'Who here is currently searching for a new car?' few people would respond. If, however, you asked, 'Who here is not 100% happy with the car they currently have?' almost everyone would respond.

There is great power in being able to identify a dormant tension people have hidden away in the back of their mind.

It seems counterintuitive but when a customer is already actively looking for a product, they are harder to sell to, not easier. People who are actively looking for something have already made up their minds and they have often set their budget. They are normally unwilling to explore a broad range of alternatives or to consider offers outside their predetermined price band.

People who are actively searching for a product or a service are also likely to buy from the most established providers. They typically go with well-known brands or the people who have won awards and have dozens of testimonials. As they fine-tune their decision, they look for signs that a business is the best of the bunch.

ASKING REVEALING QUESTIONS

When exploring a dormant desire, people tend to buy from the business that helped them uncover it. Someone who wasn't looking for a life coach will buy from the life coach who helped them to highlight an area of their life they could improve.

Those with a dormant frustration are also open to exploring a full range of options. A person who knows they want to join a golf club will look for the best golf club in their local area. A person who feels bored because they don't have any hobbies might be open to tennis, bowling, dancing, karate, rock climbing or golf.

The smartest entrepreneurs and marketing professionals sell to those with dormant needs and wants. They go looking for underlying psychological tension that hasn't yet fully formed and then they warm people up.

The key to finding a psychological tension is in asking the right questions. If you ask people about small things they are experiencing, they begin to tune into issues that need resolving. Small things can add up to big things.

A big tension someone might have could relate to their fitness, but asking directly about it might cause them to recoil. Imagine asking someone you barely know, 'Are you happy with your fitness/weight?' You won't win any new friends that way. Asking fewer encompassing questions would be a better way to start the ball rolling. Questions like 'do you work out?' or 'do you have any sporty hobbies?' would start a conversation that may reveal their deeper thoughts.

Having a series of simple, indirect questions to ask can be a powerful way to wake up the dormant frustrations or desires in those your business could help.

ACTION STEP

Get into the mind of your potential customers:

- » What dormant frustrations do your typical customers experience?

- » What desired outcomes do your typical customers secretly want?

- » What typically stops people from acting on this tension?

WARMING PEOPLE UP

When psychological tension builds, people go looking for solutions. People who are *actively* looking for something appear to buy quickly. They already have a fully formed set of ideas about what they want and how much they're willing to pay. If they see something that meets their needs and wants, they can just put it on their credit card. Within minutes, they've added it to their cart and sent it whizzing from the warehouse to their door. Not everyone is at that point, though.

When someone has a psychological tension brewing under the surface, it can take time for them to feel ready to buy something. If you're catching them early in their buying journey, remember that they still need to go through a process of learning and mentally trying on various options and solutions.

The person who is dissatisfied with working too hard in their business might not yet know if they should buy some software, hire a business coach or perhaps recruit someone onto their team. There could be dozens of ways to approach their issue.

The business that can deliver the most effective education and entertainment at this time normally wins the sale. Smart businesses know how to warm people up in an enjoyable and easy-going way. They seek to add value to someone who's exploring a purchasing decision, before asking for the sale.

Let's go back to the example of Kelly and the yoga studio that has launched classes for parents. They know that parents can't easily commit to a new hobby so they don't try to push for the sale. Instead, they share information about why and how they've designed these yoga classes to suit parents.

They have videos of parents saying that the classes are perfect for busy parents and the benefits are worthwhile. They provide a checklist for getting back into a yoga practice. There is a blog that talks about the importance of taking care of yourself, your fitness and your own energy levels as a parent. They also have podcast episodes that discuss that amazing centred feeling you get after a yoga class, and how couples with kids have a better relationship if they manage their stress. For someone who experiences these sequences of content, the decision to join the yoga studio becomes more and more obvious.

Warming people up is a science. In their research, Google discovered that people typically consume eleven pieces of content before making a purchase. They call this moment of online decision-making 'Zero Moments of Truth', or ZMOT.[3] Psychology Professor Robin Dunbar found that time and quality interactions determined how much trust and connection people experienced. His research showed that spending several hours with someone across multiple interactions in a week significantly sped up the time it took to bond.[4]

Businesses and brands can harness this idea by creating content journeys for people to go on. Using digital assets like videos, articles, images, podcasts and social networks, a business can create a trail of marketing 'breadcrumbs' that lead people to their door.

QUANTITY AND QUALITY CONTENT

When it comes to warming people up to doing business with you, quality as well as quantity is important.

Quality content is about personalisation. Content that speaks to a person directly is much more influential than generic information. If someone uses your name and talks about the exact needs you have, you are likely to respond.

Amid the flood of information we all have access to, people make snap judgements about whether something is relevant to them or not. As soon as they suspect that something isn't intended directly for them, their interest in it drops off a cliff. This is especially true in a world where we are only a click away from our favourite YouTube channels or Amazon recommendations.

72% of consumers say that they only engage with personalised messaging.[5]

The other important aspect is the quantity of content. Our experience and the research we've seen indicates that a business should have at least eleven pieces of relevant content available for people to read, watch, listen to or interact with. Some people might not need that much but many like to go deep down the rabbit hole when they discover something new.

A person considering buying a guitar may want to look at the specifications, see videos of famous people with that guitar, listen to experts playing and reviewing it, and then read customer testimonials and reviews. This process could take a few days or a few weeks and you don't want them to run out of content to engage with.

The hard part is combining the two. Having personalised content while also having a lot of content for each potential customer is hard for most businesses to achieve. Historically, the way to solve this has been to have armies of salespeople who can talk to customers and clients one-to-one, understand their situation and then make recommendations to follow up. It's expensive and beyond the reach of most small businesses.

Technology companies try to solve this with algorithms. Amazon, Spotify, YouTube and Facebook all learn about what people want and drip-feed recommendations that are personalised to each of us. This works better on some occasions than others, but, even if it only works some of the time, these businesses see a huge uplift in sales.

The holy grail is personalisation that happens automatically and can deliver dynamic recommendations to people based on their unique situation. Scorecard marketing is the tool that allows small businesses to deliver personalised content and recommendations at scale without having to hire armies of salespeople or software developers.

When people complete your scorecard, they answer a quick questionnaire or a quiz. The way they answer gives you information about them and adds a simple scoring system to their response, which makes it easy to then personalise the content they see. This dynamic content is much more engaging and effective at warming up leads.

ACTION STEP

Explore the journey your customers go through before they buy:

1. What is the missing information your potential customers typically need in order to feel more desire to buy from you?

2. What quality content do you currently have available online for people to access?

3. How do you currently discover unique information about your potential clients?

THE PRODUCT-FOR-PROSPECTS

Businesses typically have a core product or service that they offer. They work with this thing every day and become experts in it.

An accountant's core business is delivering accounting services. A business coach's core business is providing business coaching programmes. An architect's core business is designing homes. Sometimes people who work closely with something forget what it's like not to know what they know.

A dentist's core business might be teeth straightening and they might easily forget what it's like not to know what teeth straightening involves. They could forget what it's like not to know how long it takes, how effective it is and what to expect during the process. They do it every day, they are an expert and can completely disconnect from the concerns and hopes someone has when first exploring this as an option. It's easy to become complacent about the basic questions people might have.

The best way to solve this problem is to create a 'product-for-prospects'. This is a low-risk first step people can take before committing to your core product. The product-for-prospects is a packaged-up way for people to connect and learn about what you do.

The dentist could sell a 'discovery visit' to explore the possibility of 'improving your smile' as a product-for-prospects which would be appealing for the person thinking about committing to the journey.

Most professionals don't like giving away free discovery sessions because they are time-consuming and might not result in a sale. If you meet people one-to-one for free you will quickly run out of time to work with paying customers. The key to a powerful product-for-prospects is for it to be scalable. You need to create something that lots of people can happily engage with that takes up only a small amount of your time, if any.

AN *INDIRECT* APPROACH TO MARKETING

When I was a teenager, our local newspaper had an advertisement that ran every Saturday for years. It was for a local financial planner who ran a weekly workshop called 'An Introduction to Building Wealth and Having Security in Retirement'. The ad focused on the benefits of attending a two-hour workshop. Rather than trying to sell financial planning, this business pointed their marketing budget at a product-for-prospects.

The two-hour workshop typically attracted ten to thirty people each time and it was repeated for many years. People attended, they learned, then signed up with a financial planner and the business grew. Eventually, that business was sold for AU$30 million and the founder ended up on the Australian Young Rich List. The secret to successfully selling the financial planning services was to avoid selling financial planning services and to get people to engage first with the product-for-prospects.

Inspired by this example, Glen and I built our first business based on the concept of running introductory workshops. This business was a huge success because we were experts in getting people to engage with a product-for-prospects. We could identify companies trying to sell their core offer directly and radically grow their business just by promoting an introductory workshop instead.

Workshops, books, reports, events and sample packs are all great examples of scalable products-for-prospects that can engage larger groups of people, but they do each have significant downsides. All of these products-for-prospects are also one-sided. They are great for telling people about your business but they do not tell the business much about the potential customer.

A person sitting in on a workshop might be a millionaire looking to spend big or someone who's just been made redundant and is fearful about spending any money at all. You don't know who's reading your books or attending your events.

A scorecard is the perfect product-for-prospects for a customer to engage with. It asks your potential clients a series of simple, indirect questions that reveal the frustrations or desires they want to address. From their point of view, it's more personalised than a book or a workshop and it requires less time. Research clearly shows that most people are willing to give out information about themselves if it saves time and leads to personalised recommendations.

**83% of consumers are prepared to share their data
for a more personalised experience.**[6]

The worst type of product-for-prospects is a one-to-one meeting. Even though it's a great way to get to know someone, it's time-intensive and an elementary use of a professional's skills. Anyone who could be good at delivering it would be better off doing more advanced work with clients.

A better product-for-prospects is a workshop or a book – they scale, but lack the personalisation of a one-to-one meeting and don't collect much information about your prospective client. People sitting in a workshop or reading a book don't reveal much about themselves.

The scorecard stands out as the best product-for-prospects because it is scalable, collects valuable information and delivers a personalised experience. They are the ultimate first step towards a bigger sale.

ACTION STEP

Consider what it's like not to know much about your product:

1. What are the top questions people want answered before they buy from you?

2. What information do you wish more people understood so they see the full value of what you do?

EMOTION, LOGIC AND URGENCY

Even after you've warmed someone up and they've engaged with a product-for-prospects, not everyone will buy from you.

Every day thousands of people walk into an Apple Retail Store and don't buy – even though they are warm to doing business with Apple and even though they can take workshops or talk to Apple geniuses if they want to.

Let's not kid ourselves: humans are a fickle bunch who only buy things when the conditions are just right. Getting people to buy something is like launching a rocket – if things aren't exactly right, the countdown to ignition sequence won't even start.

For a sale to be made, three psychological ingredients must be present:

1. **Emotion** – People need to feel a certain way about the business they are buying from. First, they need to feel respected, understood and that a sense of trust has been established. Then they need to feel some form of emotional pay-off would be achieved by buying. Emotions are normally about the stories we tell

ourselves. These stories have heroes and villains. They have struggles and triumphs. There is often fear and greed involved.

2. **Logic** – People need to understand the practical reasons why they should buy. This normally means calculating a clear return on investment (ROI), a cost-benefit analysis or making a comparison with alternatives. Most logical arguments can be made using facts, statistics, diagrams and data.

3. **Urgency** – Even when someone understands the logic of buying and feels an emotional connection to the purchase, they must also feel that it's important to make a decision now. A sense of urgency comes when we feel that there is a cost associated with inaction. We might miss out on something we want, the purchase could become more expensive, the quality might deteriorate or the availability could dry up. Without a sense of urgency, people delay making decisions.

A business making a lot of sales has succeeded in mixing all three of these ingredients together elegantly and in the right proportions.

Emotion, logic and urgency are what customers need to feel before buying. These ingredients often form little loops of attention, engagement and action. Attention, engagement and action are what marketers need from customers so they can measure what's working.

LOGIC + EMOTION + URGENCY

A powerful marketing campaign will capture your attention with something that sparks an emotion. Then, it will engage your mind with something factual or interesting to consider. Finally, it will ask you to take an action that feels increasingly urgent.

Loops of emotion, logic and urgency can be small or they can be drawn out. You might see an ad on Facebook with an image of a beautiful couple staring romantically into each other's eyes. This sparks emotion. Then the advertising copy says, 'Romantic package holidays are on sale now. Five-star accommodation, flights and car hire all included. Daily flights to the most highly rated destinations with flight times under four hours.' This is the logical information you need to start considering this purchase. Finally, the ad might say, 'Sale ends at midnight', giving you an urgent reason to click the link and take a look at what's on offer. This advertisement contains all three elements of emotion, logic and urgency in a fast loop.

A much slower loop might be for the purchase of a new car. Billboard images on the motorway might communicate luxury, prestige, safety and status. The company website would contain detailed information about the vehicle specifications. Talking to a salesperson might reveal that there's only one left in stock with everything you want; otherwise, you'll have to join a waiting list to get it factory produced. This loop could take weeks for a customer to complete and they might not even be aware of the steps their brain went through.

ON A SCALE OF ONE TO TEN

Performance marketing is a type of marketing designed around these stages of emotion, logic and urgency that creates the right conditions for people to feel inspired to buy. This type of approach measures and optimises how much positive attention your business can get using the right emotional hook, the amount of engagement you get from people as they interact and share data about themselves and, finally, the number of people who take a desired action.

One of the ways to integrate logic and emotion is to quantify a person's situation. Have you noticed that doctors ask their patients, 'On a scale of one to ten, how painful is it?' This powerful question gets the human brain to engage emotion and logic simultaneously. The emotion is the pain and the logic is the number the patient assigns to it.

When people quantify things, they are a step closer to looking for solutions and improvements. You can ask customers to rate their levels of satisfaction with all sorts of things. As a general rule, if a customer rates something as a seven out of ten or above, it's satisfactory and won't get much attention. If it drops below a four, it's becoming unbearable and the customer will likely want to take action.

The way people view the world can also change quickly with new information. If a mechanic shows you a report that says your car tyres are dangerously close to blowing out and your brake pads are worn down below the safety standards, you will rapidly move from being broadly satisfied with your car to looking for a solution. Diagnosing someone's situation effectively and giving them a means of scoring themselves is a remarkably fast way of moving people from having a dormant dissatisfaction to an explicit desire.

A scorecard is a perfectly designed loop with all of these principles in mind.

70% of consumers feel a company's understanding of their personal needs influences their loyalty.[7]

The scorecard landing page contains emotional hooks and logical reasons to entice someone to answer a questionnaire, and the questions create engagement. At the end, the results page inspires action because it quantifies people's situations – the dynamic content speaks directly to the reader and gives them a relevant next step and a special offer.

This elegant approach is designed to create momentum and flow by integrating logic, emotion and urgency in just a few minutes. It speeds up the process of ticking all of the boxes people need so that the conditions are right to buy.

ACTION STEP

Apply this understanding of emotion, logic and urgency to your business:

1. What are the top three emotional reasons people buy from your business?

2. What are the top three logical reasons people should buy from your business?

3. Why is it sensible for people to buy from you now rather than in the future?

SCORING, RANKING AND IMPROVING

Humans have a relentless desire to score, rank, optimise and evaluate everything. Our deep-seated need to know how we rank against a consistent, unmoving set of standards is fundamental to the way we have evolved and it affects us from cradle to grave.

Receiving feedback is another deeply ingrained human need. You can kill someone's motivation for work or achievement if you refuse to give them any form of feedback on how they are progressing. Taking away the scoreboard from a sport would cause a loss of interest in playing or watching the game. A scoreboard is the culmination of logic, emotion and urgency captured and displayed as a set of numbers.

Once we can measure something, we love to optimise and improve it. It is part of our evolutionary advantage: our ancient ancestors who didn't care about measuring and improving didn't survive. We don't simply accept things as they are – we measure anything that can be measured and look for ways to improve.

With that comes a desire to rank ourselves. It's not enough to go skiing – people need to know if they are a beginner, intermediate or advanced skier. It's not enough to play golf – we need to calculate our handicap. It's not enough to run a good business – we need to know our revenue, profit, cashflow and growth numbers.

In a work environment, a hallmark of an excellent manager is one who gives great feedback to their team. They keep score of key metrics and let their team know how they're progressing and how to improve. If a manager gets this one thing right, they will be respected and admired by their peers. A manager who gives little feedback or guidance will be rejected; if their feedback is inconsistent or unfair, they will be despised.

Preschool children respond to a chart with gold stars on it. They will alter their behaviour to gain additional gold stars. CEOs of publicly traded companies use their stock price as a scoreboard and change their focus in an attempt to make that little line move slightly up the chart. Elderly people gain health and wellness benefits when they engage in measurable community activities like charity fundraising or a bridge championship. A scorecard strengthens our will to live.

A SCORING SYSTEM IS GOOD FOR BUSINESS

One of the most powerful ways to make your business and your marketing more engaging therefore is to link it to a scoring system. Scoring something has the effect of gamifying it. It draws people in, energises them and holds their attention for longer. This is all down to the primal part of our brain that believes measuring, improving and ranking are linked to survival and reproduction.

Having seen thousands of companies set up an online questionnaire, quiz or assessment, I know how people will enthusiastically engage with a set of questions that have a point system attached.

Some examples that act as powerful hooks to capture attention and get people to engage might be:

» Are you ready to find the love of your life?
   Answer these twelve questions and discover if
   you can improve your dating success.

» Is your business scalable? Answer forty questions,
   developed by business experts, and discover your
   scalability score.

» Is poor sleep damaging your health? To find out,
   answer the top twenty questions sleep experts ask you.

» Should you ask for a pay increase, change jobs or improve your skills? This scorecard will give you a clear answer on how to advance your career. Take the quiz and find out.

» Answer fifteen questions and see if your parenting style will empower your children to succeed and be happy. You will also receive three easy tips to improve, tailored to you.

When you read these headlines, part of your brain lights up and wants to know the answer. You want to know how you score and how to improve.

Before people buy your products and services, they need to see what area of their life is going to improve as a result. Once they understand what your products and services improve, they want to know where they currently rank and how far forward they could move the score by working with you.

Your customers have probably never described their desires to you in these terms, but deep inside their mind they are making calculations. What important area of life is this helping me with? How am I currently performing in this area of life? How can I improve? How much effort would it take? What impact would that effort have on my ability to survive and reproduce?

If you can make these calculations clear for people, and it stacks up, their desire to buy from you is rapidly heightened.

Beneath every purchase is a latent desire to change and improve an important area of life. Many people are not consciously aware of this, but it impacts their decisions. That hardwired desire to score and improve sits beneath every product or service we buy.

98% of marketers believe personalisation advances customer relationships.[8]

In Part Two, we'll explore a step-by-step approach to creating an online scorecard for your potential clients. It will identify a dormant desire, raise awareness of a psychological tension, give people a way to score or rank their performance and make it easy for you to warm people up to buying the right product or service.

ACTION STEP

Tune into what your customers are trying to measure and improve:

1. What important areas of life does your business improve?

2. How might someone score themselves today if they wanted to improve that area of life in the next three months?

3. What specific things does your business do that can be measured and improved?

PART TWO

SETTING UP
A SCORECARD

BUILDING YOUR SCORECARD

On paper we had just completed the most successful six weeks of our careers, but it didn't feel that way. It was 2013 and, despite making millions, our little team were on the verge of burnout.

We had just run three large Become a Key Person of Influence events in Melbourne, Sydney and Brisbane. Each event was hosted in a theatre auditorium for 600 people. With an amazing line-up of guest speakers, we held the audience's attention with a full day of stories, strategies and activities. At the end of each event, we invited people to meet with us to discuss joining our flagship Key Person of Influence Accelerator.

About 200 people from each event would book into our strategy sessions, creating two weeks of back-to-back board-room meetings starting at 8am and finishing at 6.30pm every day. By the end of the six weeks, our small, young team had generated close to AU$1.5 million in sales.

On the surface it looked glamorous – standing on a big stage in front of hundreds of people and then hosting business strategy meetings in fancy boardrooms. In reality it was intense, demanding and expensive, but we didn't have any other way.

The big events gave people information about our business and communicated our value through a powerful and memorable approach. The strategy sessions were a vital way for us to learn more about each person and make sure they were qualified for our programmes.

At the time, we couldn't see an alternative method of showcasing our value and then learning enough about people to get the right clients. We thought we had to just keep doing things the way we were and learn to accept it. Fortunately, we were wrong.

In the background, Steven Oddy, now the CEO of ScoreApp, was working on a new innovation that was about to change everything – the Key Person of Influence Scorecard.

UNPRECEDENTED RESULTS

This scorecard had a powerful landing page that communicated our value, a questionnaire to qualify people and a results page and PDF report to give people bespoke information about their situation.

In under five minutes, people found out more about us and how we could help them. We thought this would be helpful for making sales but we didn't realise it would completely transform our business.

In the first month 171 people completed the scorecard. This was followed by 181 the next month and then over 200 people in the third month. Each person told us over fifty things about themself. We knew their business size, their frustrations, their achievements and their goals. We knew more about the people we had never met than most of the people we had had a two-hour strategy session with face to face.

It didn't take long to achieve a steady stream of 500+ people per month taking the scorecard. Those people received an automatic invitation to attend a strategy session and started booking themselves in. When we met with people, they almost always had a printout of their scorecard report. They were excited about engaging with us to talk about how to improve their scores.

Rather than having to run big events costing tens of thousands of dollars, we channelled that money into promoting our scorecards. More scorecards were filled in, more strategy session bookings came in automatically and more and more people joined our accelerator programme. It was consistent, manageable and enjoyable. We weren't burning out our team with intense campaigns and we were exceeding our sales targets.

The ScoreApp scorecard is now more advanced and more effective than the one we launched back in 2014. It contains all of the learnings and strategies we've developed since then.

SCOREAPP

We are about to start building your scorecard step by step. If you haven't done so already, create an account with ScoreApp.com. You can create a free trial account using this link: www.scoreapp.com/book-trial

If this approach turns out not to be for you, you can easily cancel your trial at any time and it will have cost you nothing. There are no long-term contracts.

If it works for your business, you'll pay a monthly fee that is tiny in comparison to the value of the qualified leads you'll get. As a customer of ScoreApp, you'll also be part of our community of business owners and marketing managers who are using this approach. It's a powerful way to learn and improve in a fun environment.

To make an effective digital scorecard, you'll need to get just four things right, and ScoreApp seamlessly creates these for you:

1. A beautiful **landing page** that clearly communicates your value and the reason to complete a short questionnaire.

2. A **questionnaire with a point-scoring system** that asks people qualifying questions to establish whether they could benefit from what you have to offer.

3. A **results page** that shows people how they scored and gives them personalised recommendations (you can also deliver this as a PDF download).

4. A **sales and marketing approach** that includes leads, data insights and tools to get people to complete your scorecard and allows you to follow up the warm leads.

Here's what people say about ScoreApp:

'ScoreApp and LinkedIn are a match made in heaven.' **— Helen Pritchard, LinkedIn training specialist**

'ScoreApp is at the cutting-edge of this digital revolution and accelerating the ability we all have to build better relationships with our audiences, and faster than we ever could before in a digital setting.' **— Josh Smith, digital marketing expert**

'It generates an abundance of great leads. If I could only recommend ONE tool for growing a fitness business, it would be ScoreApp.' **— Jamie Alderton, fitness industry influencer**

'I see countless marketing ideas and strategies – scorecard marketing stands out. This is a great innovation that combines data analytics with the psychological principles that get people excited to buy. This book takes you step by step through the process of getting your first scorecard campaign up and running successfully.' **— Allan Dib, bestselling author of *The 1-Page Marketing Plan***

FREQUENTLY ASKED QUESTIONS

How long does it take to set up a scorecard?

Most people who use a ScoreApp template are set up within an hour. You might then want to tweak and improve your scorecard as you get feedback from your customers. It's not dissimilar to setting up a LinkedIn profile, you can easily get the basics done and then add to it over time.

The most important thing is that it starts giving you back time. Lead generation and qualification is one of the most expensive and time-consuming jobs in any business. The little bit of time you invest setting up an automated marketing system like ScoreApp will pay huge dividends in time and money.

Do I need to have basic coding skills?

You don't need any coding skills to use ScoreApp. If you are comfortable using software like Google Docs or setting up a social media profile, you will be comfortable using ScoreApp. If you get stuck, we have real humans who can help you (just click the Help button on the bottom-right of the portal). We also have a community on Facebook where you can ask questions and get ideas from other ScoreApp clients.

What you do need is some creativity. You'll need to come up with an engaging way of describing what you do and asking people about their situation. After that, you'll want to find fun ways to give people insights and get them buying from your business. If you already have paying customers, you have the raw materials you need to succeed with ScoreApp.

What if it doesn't work for me?

If ScoreApp isn't performing, there are many ways to improve your scorecard so you generate leads. Asking questions in our ScoreApp Facebook group will get helpful responses. You can also watch case studies and see examples of high-performing scorecards. If you're still not convinced, you can cancel ScoreApp at any time.

The businesses that struggle with ScoreApp are those that are not clear about the value they offer to clients and the specific problems they solve. If you are clear about what you can do for a customer and why it's important, you are likely to succeed with ScoreApp.

If it works so well, why is it so cheap?

Lead generation is an expensive part of any business. Most businesses are used to paying big money for anything that helps. Many leading software tools cost several thousand dollars per year on top of expert-lead setup costs. Advertising budgets often run into the tens of thousands per month. ScoreApp is a laser-focused tool designed for small businesses to harness the power of data. We want it to be affordable for the majority of businesses.

Won't everyone have a scorecard soon?

Millions of businesses now have a podcast, YouTube channel or book that they use to promote what they do, and these tools are still effective. At the time of writing, only a few thousand businesses globally are using ScoreApp.

Still not sure if it would work for you? Take the Scorecard Readiness Assessment to check if your business would benefit from scorecard marketing: www.scoreapp. com/quizready

STEP 1:
YOUR LANDING PAGE

Imagine a perfect potential client for your business is on LinkedIn and they see a post you've written. Something about it catches their attention and they click on a link to the scorecard you've mentioned, arriving at a landing page.

The landing page is the first thing your potential clients will see. It's not the front page of your normal website, it's a dedicated page designed to get people to complete your scorecard. It has one clear objective – to get people to start a questionnaire.

Your landing page communicates your credibility and gives people a clear pathway to something they want. It's nicely designed, there are friendly faces of real people and there are desirable bonuses listed for people who complete the questionnaire. There's a nice big button that says 'Start the Quiz' or 'Discover Your Score'.

Your perfect client thinks, 'Well this only takes a few minutes, I'm curious to know what my score would be – I'll answer a few questions and this will tell me something I'd like to know.' They click the button and your landing page has successfully done its job.

To achieve this, you need to complete the following four simple steps:

1. Create a concept

2. Select a template

3. Improve the landing page

4. Start the quiz

1. CREATE A CONCEPT

Your scorecard concept is based on what your perfect potential customers would want to score themselves on.

A relationship therapist's clients would want to score themselves for the quality of their relationship. They might complete the 'Happy Marriage Scorecard' or the 'Better Relationship Quiz'.

A cybersecurity expert would have potential clients looking to identify their IT security threats. They would engage with a landing page that said, 'Can you improve your IT security? Take the Cybersecurity Scorecard.'

A fitness trainer's potential clients want to lose weight and feel great. Their potential clients would connect with a landing page that said, 'Are you ready to lose weight and feel great? Take the scorecard to discover how to speed up your results.'

What would your potential customers want to engage with? What scorecard would they want to complete to know if you can help them?

Some scorecards help people move towards something they want. The concept is about achieving a goal and getting a prize: for example, the 'Grow Your Business Scorecard' or the 'Run Your First Marathon Scorecard'.

Some scorecards help to remove a pain or frustration. For example, 'Want to reduce your work stress? Take this scorecard' or 'Avoid being hacked – take this quiz for personalised recommendations to reduce your risks' are both concepts based on removing potential pain.

Other approaches that work well are about being ready to begin something, like a preflight checklist. Some examples could be, 'Are you ready to buy your first home? Take this scorecard' or 'Should you buy a franchise? Complete this questionnaire to see if you are suitable.'

One more example that many people engage with is discovering which category they fit into. For example, 'Are you an introvert or an extrovert? Take this quiz to find out' or

'Discover your natural leadership style – complete this quiz and find out your leader profile.'

Finally, sometimes people want to test their knowledge. They answer a quiz to see how many questions they can get right. For example, 'Test your property investing knowledge – take the quiz to see if you are up to date' or 'Do you know the latest advertising trends? Test your expertise with this short quiz.'

If you've produced content for your business in the past, you might already have a good concept you're known for. If you already have a book, YouTube channel or podcast, you should definitely have a scorecard that goes with it. Not only will this give your viewers, readers and listeners something to do, but it will also identify them to you. The best leads you'll ever get are people who are engaging with your content and then happily signalling their interest by completing a scorecard.

ACTION STEP

What do you think your potential clients might want to score? Fill in the blanks to explore a few options:

- » Are you ready to...................?
- » What type of..................are you?
- » Improve your...................
- » Reduce unwanted...................
- » How good is your..................?
- » Test your knowledge on..................

PRO TIP

Come up with a few concepts and ask your followers on social media which they prefer. You can use a poll or just ask people to comment on LinkedIn, Twitter, Facebook or Instagram.

For example, you could post:

'I'm developing an online assessment for people who plan to run a marathon. Which option do you prefer?'

Option 1. 'Are you ready to run your first marathon? Take this scorecard.'

Option 2. 'The Marathon Runner Scorecard – Are you ready to reduce your finish time?'

Option 3. 'The Marathon Runner Checklist – Are you training effectively to run pain-free?'

2. SELECT A TEMPLATE

ScoreApp has plenty of templates to choose from. They are designed by experts to be effective at capturing attention, communicating value and getting people to take action. Each template can be easily edited. You can change the text, images and colours with a few clicks.

Use the template as a starting point for creating a scorecard that is unique to your business. Look for a design you feel suits your business – something similar to your website or your brochures, or that fits with the style you want to be known for.

Don't worry about the specific text, images or colours; they are all easily changed. It's also easy to start again with a new template if you change your mind.

ACTION STEP

Log in to your account at ScoreApp.com, click on the button that says 'Create Scorecard' and choose a template that catches your eye (don't overthink it).

PRO TIP

You don't have to use a template if you want to design something that is more unique to your business. If you're comfortable with websites like WordPress, Canva or Wix, you'll have the skills to design landing pages from scratch in ScoreApp.

---

3. IMPROVE THE LANDING PAGE

Great landing pages make people feel comfortable engaging further. They create feelings of desire to get started – to click the call-to-action button that initiates the questionnaire. A great landing page gives clarity about how someone will benefit from your scorecard and why your business is credible. It also creates a feeling of connection with your perfect customer. Clarity, credibility and connection are key, followed by the call to action (CTA).

Clarity is about articulating the benefits your scorecard offers people. Tell people specifically what your scorecard will help them to improve or the stresses it will remove. On your landing page include sentences like, 'This health and fitness scorecard will improve four key areas – you'll improve your diet, get better results in the gym, have more confidence and achieve deeper sleep.'

Don't assume that people automatically know what you know; instead, list all of the things that they stand to gain if they start this journey. Clarify the pain points that could be removed if they gain more insights and focus.

To drive home the value, you could offer additional bonuses for completing the scorecard. Perhaps give them a free copy of a book, a ticket to an event, or a consultation. Not only will they have the personalised recommendations your scorecard offers, but they will also gain valuable resources as well.

It's important to tell people that the scorecard is quick and easy to complete. You don't want them thinking they have to sit a forty-five-minute exam. Let them know on the landing page what to expect; for example, 'It typically takes less than three minutes to answer all twenty simple questions.'

Credibility is the next vital ingredient. Remember that most people who see your landing page don't know you well. They don't know if you are experienced or a novice; they aren't sure if they should trust you.

Tell people about your experience, your research and your awards. You could say, 'This scorecard is based on fifteen years of experience working with over 1,000 businesses. Our team have won multiple awards and been part of academic research projects. We are trusted by household name brands.'

Sharing your credibility is not about being boastful or self-obsessed. It's the opposite: you are giving people the information they need to be able to evaluate that you are a trusted source of information and advice. It's important to your potential clients to know more about you and your background. They want to trust you, so give them tangible reasons why they can.

Connection is the final ingredient of an effective landing page. People look at the landing page to get a sense or a feeling about whether it is designed for them or not. The design of the page is important – the images, colours and fonts all communicate something about you.

By glancing at a page, it should be easy to see if it is designed for corporate professionals, families, couples, fitness enthusiasts or whoever you are targeting. Do you want to show how vibrant and energising your business is? Then make sure you choose colours and images that are vibrant and energising.

Connection is also about eye contact and smiles. One of the best ways to get people to feel a greater connection with your landing page is to put a photo of you or your team on the page. This immediately reassures someone that real people are behind this business. You can boost the effectiveness of most landing pages with a quality, smiling profile photo.

ScoreApp makes it easy to add images to your landing page from your own image library or to choose from a royalty-free image library that's built into the platform. Make sure you choose pictures that show people what your business does and, more importantly, what your customers achieve as a result.

Do your customers want to see pictures of gym equipment or people who have improved their fitness? Would they be encouraged by an image of someone coaching a client or of someone who now has the career they dreamed of? Do they want to see pictures of your developers coding away at their screen or your clients launching their new online store and getting new business? Most people engage more with images of people like themselves achieving a desired result.

ACTION STEP

Write the text that you want to use on your landing page. Include a description of what your scorecard helps people to improve and why it's a valuable use of time. Be sure to include your bio or your company's story as a way of showing your credibility.

PRO TIP

A professional designer or photographer can create unique images that truly represent your brand.

---

4. START THE QUIZ

Everything on the landing page should lead towards one out-come – you want people to start the scorecard by clicking a button and entering their information. ScoreApp automatically makes these buttons big and obvious on the page. Often, you'll have a call-to-action button both at the top of the page and at the bottom so people can always see it.

The call-to-action button should say something like 'Start the Scorecard' or 'Answer the Fifteen Questions Now' or 'Begin the Quiz'. Experiment with different ways of asking people to click through to begin your scorecard but if you've been clear with the value and shown that you're credible, and if they feel a connection to your business, they'll engage.

ACTION STEP

Get your landing page set up in ScoreApp. Once you've spent some time on the text, images, colours and fonts ask a trusted friend or colleague for feedback. In particular, are they clear about the value it offers? Do they understand why you are a reliable source of information?

Just by looking at the page, do they get a sense that your business cares and real people are behind this business?

PRO TIP

When choosing images, pick the ones that represent the result people want, not the process of getting there.

THE LEAD FORM

When someone starts a scorecard, they begin by putting their details into a lead capture form. It will typically ask them for their name and email address. You can easily set up the lead form to capture any other information you want.

Many ScoreApp scorecards use the lead form to collect a phone number, location and job title. It's also possible to create a drop-down menu option on the lead form to ask people for information about their current situation – for example, 'What level of experience do you have?' or 'What is the size of your organisation?' You can make these questions 'optional' so people don't have to select an answer, or you can make them 'required'.

Even if a person doesn't complete the questionnaire, you will have the information they provide in the lead form. You can even set up an 'abandon email' that automatically goes out if someone doesn't finish your questionnaire – it lets them pick up where they left off.

PRO TIP

Some ScoreApp clients want to let people complete the questionnaire first and then enter their details at the end. This can be more effective if you want the questionnaire data more than you want the person's details. When you put the lead form at the end of the questionnaire, people will see a basic display of their overall score but they will have to fill in the lead form to see their full results and recommendations.

GDPR compliance

The General Data Protection Regulation (2016) is a regulation in EU law on data protection and privacy in the European Union and the European Economic Area. The most important aspects are that you collect data with people's consent, store their data safely, delete data if requested and you are able to let people know what data you are keeping about them if they require. ScoreApp works with a leading law firm to help you comply with these laws easily and automatically. Many of the important aspects of GDPR compliance are built into our systems and if there are major changes, we take steps to address them.

There are comprehensive checklists and other information at www.gdpr.eu

THE ONLY TRUTH IS THE RESULTS

You want people to stop what they are doing and start your questionnaire. Some highly effective landing pages are short and sharp, other high-converting landing pages have thousands of words and dozens of images. I have seen a landing page with less than 100 words and one image succeed at getting people to click the button and start the quiz.

Creating a landing page is not a competition judged by expert writers and art critics. It's your customers who cast the votes with their actions. Measuring 'conversion' – how many people arrive at your landing page versus the number of people who start your scorecard – is very useful.

PRO TIP

ScoreApp allows you to create several versions of a landing page and then shows you the conversion statistics so you can decide which version is the best.

'Making a few tweaks to our landing page massively improved conversions – more than double actually! I asked people in the ScoreApp Facebook group what they would change and I got some great feedback. After these changes were made, people were much clearer about why they should take my scorecard.'

— Jonathan Bird, Delivered Social

CASE STUDY: BUNKIE LIFE

A 'Bunkie' originates from Ontario, Canada and is a small log cabin that can be built in a weekend without a permit or second mortgage, and can be used as a guest house, office or Airbnb.

Bunkie Life was founded in 2018 by avid Bunkie user David Fraser and helps families create extra space for more meaningful connection.

THE CHALLENGE

Bunkie Life burst onto the scene with a unique product and a powerful media strategy. Although the enquiries started to roll in, it was clear to David that there was a lot of excitement but not enough people were in a position to buy.

With the business still in its infancy and a Bunkie a relatively unknown concept, it was imperative that the Bunkie Life team were equally as focused on education as they were on promotion. That way they could set expectations, gauge buyer readiness and manage the incoming enquiries effectively.

THE SOLUTION

David created the scorecard 'Are You Ready for the Bunkie Life?' with the clear strategy of creating an evergreen asset that segmented their incoming leads by testing people against their knowledge, situation and lifestyle.

https://bunkielife.scoreapp.com

Armed with information and data on their strengths and weaknesses, Bunkie Life added each person to an email nurture campaign in accordance with their score. The most promising prospects received a call from the Bunkie team while the others were fed free educational material that would help them along their journey. Win-win.

PROMOTION

Bunkie Life use video and media to their advantage, with David's family at the heart of his business. His young daughter, Evie, is one of the stars of the show.

Setting up his scorecard helped David to identify the top twenty questions that he needed answers for to ascertain if someone would be a viable Bunkie Lifer. This saved a huge amount of time and allowed the business to turn the marketing tap on.

THE RESULTS

One of their latest campaigns (Jan/Feb 2022) saw over 13,000 leads and climbing with an almost unmatched 97% conversion rate.

They've tripled revenue year-on-year since launching their scorecard, growing from £800K in 2019 to £2.4 million in 2020 and £7 million in 2021. In 2021 Bunkie Life secured £1 million in Dragons' Den investment from all five Dragons.

Over 50% of all sales have come through the scorecard. That equates to £3.5 million in 2021.

STEP 2: A QUESTIONNAIRE

Your perfect client has seen the landing page, they like it, they trust it and they want more. They click the button and start the questionnaire, which should ask questions that get them thinking, evaluate their current behaviour and reveal information about their situation.

This is a win-win process of discovery. By evaluating their own thinking, knowledge and behaviour, the person completing the scorecard can gain valuable insights and get closer to achieving a goal.

For you, this process gathers useful facts about your prospective client. The information will help you to connect with them and make personalised recommendations. It will allow you to make more sales, to the right type of clients, every time.

71% of consumers feel frustrated when a shopping experience is impersonal.[9]

The questionnaire should be fast, fun and give you the facts you need. Your scorecard should take no more than a few minutes to complete, with questions that are thoughtful and easy to answer.

A CREATIVE APPROACH TO ASKING THE RIGHT QUESTIONS

To begin the process of writing your questionnaire, let's start with the idea of a checklist.

Imagine you are about to set off on a long holiday. Before you leave the house, you want to make sure you haven't forgotten anything important. Wouldn't it be helpful to have the perfect checklist from an expert traveller available to you? An example might be:

» Do you have your passport?   Yes/No

» Have you printed your travel itinerary?   Yes/No

» Have you packed your running shoes?   Yes/No

» Have you thrown away any food that could go off while you are away?   Yes/No

» Have you booked transport to your hotel?   Yes/No

As you run through the list, you identify things you need to do or you put your mind at ease.

You can apply this idea to writing your first scorecard. Your clients want to get to a destination too. They want to achieve a goal or remove a stress. You are more experienced and knowledgeable than they are in this area and you can ask questions to discover if they are on track.

The best types of questions are usually simple yes or no questions, such as: 'Have you...?', 'Do you...?', 'Did you...?', 'Are there...?', 'Does it...?', 'Will you...?' You want to ask people questions they can answer without having to go away and check.

If someone wanted to get better sleep, you might ask them these questions before trying to help them improve their situation:

- » Do you go to bed at the same time each night?   Yes/No

- » Do you often drink coffee after midday?   Yes/No

- » Is your room cool, quiet and dark in the morning? Yes/No

- » Do you typically use technology like iPads and computer games after 8pm?   Yes/No

- » Do you often eat a heavy meal later than 8pm?   Yes/No

Answering 'no' to most of these questions would produce a bad 'sleep score' and probably indicate a person is not getting a good night's sleep. Depending on how they answer, you can identify what might be causing this.

ACTION STEP

Think about a typical result your clients are trying to achieve when they work with you. What yes or no questions could you ask someone to evaluate their current likelihood of getting this result? Try to think of ten questions for your checklist.

PRO TIP

Any nonfiction book can be turned into a scorecard simply by asking one or two questions for each of the chapters. A scorecard becomes a perfect accompaniment for your book and turns your readers into hot leads you can connect with.

Here are some examples of effective questions:

Health and fitness checklist

»   Do you work out in a gym three or more times per week?

»   Do you actively try to improve your cardio strength?

»   Do you lift weights that feel quite heavy for you?

»   Do you plan your meals for the week in advance?

»   Do you know how many calories you need to consume each day to reach your goal?

»   Do you track your calories each day?

Business growth checklist

» Do you use a proven process to get the best talent when you hire people?

» Is your team aligned to a few important goals?

» Does every member of your team know exactly how to measure a successful week?

» Do you regularly train your people to improve their skills?

» Are you comfortable letting someone go if they aren't performing?

» Do you have a marketing budget based on an allowable cost per sale?

OTHER WAYS TO ASK

There's more than one way to ask a question in ScoreApp.

You can ask people to rate something on a sliding scale. Rather than a simple 'yes' or 'no', you might want to know the answer to, 'To what degree do you feel...?' or 'On a scale, how important is... to you?' or 'How often does your business...?' These answers give people a chance to tell you more nuanced information about themselves.

You can also give people checkboxes. This could be useful if you want to ask a question like, 'What software applications do you use regularly?' because then you can give them a list of options to select. People can tick as many of these checkboxes as they like, or leave them all blank.

Similar to checkboxes are radio buttons. These only allow people to select one answer from the list. You might ask the question, 'Which best describes your current situation?' and then give a few options to choose one from.

You could also ask an open question like 'What has stopped you in the past from trying XYZ?', although I don't recommend asking many of these because they slow people down.

PRO TIP

A fun way to make your questions more engaging is to change the label on each answer. Rather than 'Yes' you could put 'That's me' or 'Totally!' Instead of 'No' you could put 'No – but I want to try it'. I like to add an option to answer with something like 'I want to get help with this' or 'I need to discuss this'. If people click that button, it's easy to give them a call and discuss it; after all, they said they want to.

There are a few types of questions that put people off and frequently result in them abandoning your scorecard altogether. These include:

» **Overly salesy questions** – Questions like 'Are you ready to buy now?' or 'If we can get you the right solution, would you like to purchase it?' Trust that if they are filling in the scorecard, they are interested in a solution.

» **Leading the witness** – A question like 'Are you frustrated that you don't have a qualified and reliable sales skills trainer?' is too obvious. You might swap this with 'Are you frustrated that you sometimes don't know how to handle a difficult sales objection from a customer?'

» **Things people have to go and check** – The answer to 'Does your phone plan come up for renewal in the next three months?' isn't something most people know from memory so they would have to go away and check – most of the time they won't come back. Instead, keep questions simple; for example, 'Have you recently signed up for a new phone plan or upgraded your phone?'

» **Expert knowledge** – Remember that your perfect customers are probably not up to date on the trends and terminology that you take for granted. If you ask, 'Do you practise progressive overload during your weights training?', most people won't understand the question. It's best to write your questions so that anyone sitting in a coffee shop would be able to understand.

ACTION STEP

Show your questions to someone outside of your industry and ask them if any seem hard to understand,
irrelevant or too pushy.

ADDING CATEGORIES

The questionnaire asks people about their behaviour, attitudes
and results. To create a more advanced questionnaire, you
should have some categories that the questions relate to. For
example, if you wanted to run a checklist on someone's health
goals you might have categories like diet, exercise, sleep and
mindset.

For each of the categories, you can have questions that
relate specifically to that thing. If you have a category called
'Nutrition' you could have five questions about things that
relate to the way someone eats. The same scorecard could also
have five questions that relate to the category 'Exercise'.

If you ask questions for each of these categories, you might
discover that someone is stronger in some categories than
others. They might have a great diet but not exercise often.

Imagine you want to discover if someone is an extrovert
or an introvert. These are just two categories of personality so
you ask questions that help identify which personality type
someone is. If you asked, 'Do you feel energised after meeting
several new people?' the answer 'yes' would lean towards the

extrovert category and the answer 'no' would indicate more introverted tendencies.

Most of the time, there will be between two and seven categories worth measuring. Here are some examples:

» Business Growth – Marketing, Operations, Administration, Leadership

» Relationships – Communication, Conflict Resolution, Connection

» Happiness – Friendships, Stress, Support

» Personality – Introvert, Extrovert

» Running Style – Sprinter, Endurance

» Restaurant Quality – Food, Service, Atmosphere

'People are more willing to answer questions on my scorecard than in person. Even if I spoke to them for an hour, I don't think I would find out as much as the scorecard questions reveal in a few minutes.'

— Philip Calvert, LinkedIn and marketing keynote speaker

ACTION STEP

What categories typically relate to your scorecard concept? Come up with a few variations and ask trusted colleagues which ones are worth measuring.

PRO TIP

Create a 'signature method' for achieving a goal. You've probably seen books that have a signature method like *7 Habits of Highly Effective People* by Steven R Covey[10] or *Rich Dad's Cashflow Quadrant* by Robert Kiyosaki.[11] If you can develop your own approach, this becomes the perfect framework for your scorecard categories.

HOW MANY CATEGORIES AND HOW MANY QUESTIONS?

When it comes to scorecards, there are three main ways for people to use them and each has a questionnaire that is designed for a purpose.

Cold leads into warm leads – 1 to 3 categories, 8 to 15 questions

If you are using your scorecard as a first interaction, it's best to keep it punchy. You might run ads on Facebook or Google which lead straight to your landing page, and the people who arrive there don't know much about you. They aren't going to spend much time there and they don't trust you yet, so focus your scorecard on answering a question that doesn't require time or trust to understand. At the end of your scorecard, suggest more content for people to watch, read or listen to and then follow up with a thoughtful email.

Examples

> » 'Are you ready for a serious relationship? Take this quick quiz and find out if you are ready to date and relate with the right person.'

> » 'Sell your home for the maximum price! Answer twelve questions on this digital scorecard to see if you are ready to get the top price when your house sells.'

> » 'Which holiday destination should you choose? Answer eight questions and discover the best place for your next getaway.'

Warm leads into sales meetings – 3 to 7 categories, 20 to 50 questions

If the people arriving at your scorecard are already warm, you can engage with them more; you can ask questions and give them more detailed feedback. If someone has read your book, attended your workshop, watched your video or listened to your podcast, they are already warm to doing business with you and the scorecard is going to prepare them for a perfect sales meeting. Ask all the questions that would help you both create a quality working relationship. When you deliver the results, give people all the information they need to consider prior to a sales call, send them a polite follow-up email with the report and make it easy for them to book a time to have a sales conversation.

Examples

- » '24Assets Scorecard – You've read the book, now apply the learnings. Complete this scorecard to test where you are strong and where you should focus your effort.'

- » 'Pitch Ready Scorecard – Find out if your business is ready to raise money from professional investors, on the best terms.'

- » 'Professional DJ Scorecard – Measure yourself on the five areas of achieving success that will fill the dance floor as a professional, high-earning DJ.'

Clients into raving fans – 3 to 10 categories, 30 to 150 questions

Some people are using scorecards with their paying clients as a way to start the relationship. Before they work with a client, they get them to complete an extensive scorecard that highlights every detail that could need some attention. The scorecard results guide the relationship and the work that gets done. At regular intervals, the client can take the assessment again to see how far they have progressed and improved.

One ScoreApp client used their mental health scorecard to win a large engagement with a big team. Each member of the team started by completing a scorecard that measured their strategies for dealing with stress at work and their attitudes to their working environment. After three months of training and support, the same team retook the scorecard and the results were impressive. Neither the individuals nor the management could believe how far they had come in just ninety days. Needless to say, it led to more work because the data showed how successful the programme was.

Examples

>> 'The Wheel of Life Satisfaction Assessment – Answer 70 questions and identify the areas of greatest impact to improve your life in the next 90 days.'

>> 'The Executive 360 Scorecard – This comprehensive assessment will support you and your executive coach to plan and implement change.'

» 'The IT Security Annual Check-in – This questionnaire is designed to highlight areas of risk in your IT systems and should be revisited at least every 12 months.'

SCORING THE ANSWERS

ScoreApp lets you ask questions and then score the answers. You can assign or deduct points for each answer given. These points are automatically calculated on the results page and those who complete the scorecard receive personalised information based on how they scored.

Assigning points is a fun way to give your questionnaire more impact and meaning, as you decide what's important for moving people towards their goal. To keep things simple, assign one point for each answer that does this. If you want to be more advanced, you can deduct points for the opposite and you could even consider weighting your answers with extra points for the content that has greater impact.

When I was creating the 'Key Person of Influence Scorecard', I already had the big concept, based on my book of the same name. I also knew the categories because, in my book, I had a method called the 5Ps – Pitching, Publishing, Products, Profile and Partnerships – which were perfect to measure people against.

The parts I had to get creative with were the questions and the point-scoring system. When I was coming up with questions for the 'Publish' category, I asked questions like:

> » Have you written a blog or an article in the last month?

> » Have you published academic research?

> » Have you written a book that relates to your current business?

It's easy to see that the answers to these questions shouldn't be weighted the same. Writing a blog this month is not the same as writing a book. To keep it fair, I assigned more points for writing a book than for the academic papers, and fewer points for the blog or article than for the academic papers.

ACTION STEP

Log in to your ScoreApp portal and create some categories to score people on. Under each category, write three to seven questions that assess how someone is performing in that category. Next to each answer, assign some points. Typically, people assign (or deduct) between one and five points, depending on the significance of the question and answer.

PRO TIP

If you want to add some questions that don't relate to any of the categories, ScoreApp has a section called 'Uncategorised Questions'. These questions could relate to overall performance or general issues. This is also a good place to add one or two cheeky questions you want to know the answer to. You might want to ask something like 'Does your company have a budget for XYZ?' or 'How urgently do you want to start making changes?' These qualifying questions are pure gold when the time comes to talk to people and make sales.

GET PEOPLE THINKING

The questionnaire should be designed to be fast, fun and focused on exploring people's problems and results. Any question that brings latent or dormant desires to the surface is especially powerful.

Imagine a CEO who doesn't spend much time thinking about cybersecurity threats answering a scorecard that asks things like:

» If your Customer Relationship Management (CRM) system was hacked, would you know the urgent steps to take?

» If a scammer locked you out of your own computer systems and threatened to delete everything unless they received a payment, would you know what to do?

» Are your employees trained on how to spot fake social media accounts and suspicious emails?

With a few short questions, that CEO has gone from almost zero interest in cybersecurity to being highly aware of some shortcomings that need to be addressed.

The questions you ask are not just things you want to know about people; these are the things you want your potential customers to tune into.

CASE STUDY: SCALE ACADEMY

Carolin and her team work with service-based business owners to scale their companies with ease and elegance. ScoreApp has become their lead generation tool, positioning them as the experts with a robust system for generating highly qualified leads.

THE CHALLENGE

Carolin Soldo and her team were looking for a solution that would assess businesses on their ability to scale. There were two key reasons: to offer a more tailored approach that led with value, and to be more efficient with the lead generation process.

Although highly proficient in generating leads from marketing and ads, the Scale Academy felt the conversion rate would improve with a more end-to-end automated solution that led with value first.

THE SOLUTION

By creating the 'Business Growth Scorecard', the Scale Academy have been able to assist coaches and businesses by exposing the gaps and offering a solution that will save them time and money and boost their revenue. The leads and prospects coming through the scorecard allow a clearer perspective on their current situation that gives Carolin's team the necessary data to make an immediate impact.

By harnessing the data, Scale Academy can follow up with the highest quality leads first while automatically adding those that might not be ready to buy yet into an email nurture campaign.

It is an end-to-end lead strategy that leads with value.

PROMOTION

When going live, Scale Academy strategically created a launch around their scorecard to generate excitement and interest. For the launch, they organised a free live stream and promoted this to their existing email list, created posts on social media and spoke about it during their webinars.

This generated lots of awareness and gave their existing network another opportunity to explore how to work with them.

As well as their highly successful launch, they maximise their marketing efforts with both paid and organic marketing to promote their scorecard.

Carolin creates lots of highly valuable content on YouTube and opts for a clear CTA of 'Take the Scorecard'. Check it out here: www.youtube.com/watch?v=qzDzGX0jq-M

One of their greatest successes with generating leads has been through paid ads on Facebook. On the ad itself they lead with the messaging 'Get a Complete Business Action Plan in 10 Minutes or Less'. This prompts those who are interested to click the ad and land on the scorecard landing page.

PRO TIP

After some testing, Carolin learned that using the same picture on both her ad and her scorecard landing page actually generated a higher conversion rate. It builds trust and credibility that the ad is not leading to a different website than what was promised.

THE RESULTS

Over 3,000 people completed their scorecard in the first year, generating an average of 200–400 leads

per month. On average, people completed the scorecard in 4:51 minutes, with a 20% email opt-in rate and
a 20% follow-up booking rate.

All this resulted in over six figures a year in revenue
directly linked to their scorecard.

STEP 3: THEIR RESULTS

Your perfect client saw the landing page and it got their interest. They've answered the questionnaire and now they want to see their results. In the background, ScoreApp has been keeping track of all their responses and adding up the scores.

This is the magical moment when all is revealed. It's the reason someone started the scorecard in the first place and, if you set this up right, you will have delivered some real value to a client, with your business running on autopilot.

At the end of the questionnaire, the ScoreApp system shows people their personalised results. They will see:

» Their **overall score** – This is the score based on how they answered all of the questions regardless of category.

» Their **category scores** – This is how they scored for each of the categories regardless of how they did with the questions that didn't relate to that category. It's quite common for someone to get an average overall score with a category that is quite strong and another one that is weak.

» **Dynamic content** – This is text or media that is shown to them based on how they scored.

Additionally, people will receive an email so they can easily revisit their results. The advanced features of ScoreApp also allow you to set up a PDF version of their results that is emailed to them, full of dynamic content based on how they scored.

All of this sounds pretty complicated to set up but you can create dynamic content quickly and easily. You start by setting up scoring tiers.

SCORING TIERS

To give people context, and to allow the ScoreApp system to display the right dynamic content, you adjust the scoring tiers. These put the scores into typical ranges that are similar and ScoreApp will deliver content to people based on that range or tier.

The default is low, medium and high tiers; however, you can have as many tiers as you like. You can also name the tiers anything that you want, such as 'beginner, intermediate and advanced' or 'start-up, scale-up, performer and unicorn'.

It is a good idea to tweak and adjust your questionnaire so that your ideal client can see they have room to improve. If everyone easily gets a perfect score, your scorecard will have confirmed that they do *not* need your offer. If people score too low, they might feel that they aren't ready to work with you yet.

The perfect scenario is that your ideal potential client answers thought-provoking questions and gets a score that says 'strong foundations, with plenty of room to improve'.

'Scorecards are different to surveys because the person filling in a survey doesn't usually get anything back in return. A scorecard, however, returns a useful, personalised report as soon as the questions are complete. This means a business can automate the process of gaining credibility, understanding a customer, building brand affinity and giving advice.'

— Jodie Cook, Forbes.com

ACTION STEP

In your ScoreApp platform, set up your scoring tiers and give each a label that suits your business or industry.

PRO TIP

You can set the tiers at whatever scores you want. You can make a low score 0–40%, a medium could be 41–89% and a high score could be 90–100% (if you want to make the high score hard to achieve). Some people create five to ten tiers and some people use the tiers to distinguish between two things like 'adventure seeker' or 'luxury traveller'. Put some thought into the labels and the psychology behind your tiers. Remember that people buy when they feel tension, and don't underestimate people's natural drive to improve and achieve the high score.

DYNAMIC CONTENT

Once you have set your scoring tiers, you can easily create the dynamic content you want to show people for each tier.

For example, if someone scores in the low tier you might want to say something like, 'It looks like this area could use some improvement. Our team would love to talk to you about ways to achieve this. Here's a list of easy first steps to try…'

If, however, someone scores high on the same scorecard, you probably want to say something like, 'Well done, it looks like this area is strong. Your focus should be on maintaining high standards and only taking advice from people who specialise in working at advanced levels. Our team are skilled and experienced at working with people like yourself and can arrange a free consultation to discuss our professional approach.'

Dynamic content requires you to put some thought into how you want to communicate with each recipient at each of your scoring tiers. Your goal is to provide them with quality insights that are tailored to them.

Personalised calls to action convert 202% better than default or standard calls to action.[12]

Dynamic content is not limited to the text people see in their overall scores and their category scores – you can use dynamic content with videos, special offers and even the customer testimonials you show to people. If you know someone is a beginner, you can show them a video that is targeted at a beginner and a customer testimonial from someone you helped from an early stage. If someone is intermediate, you can adjust the videos and testimonials to match.

ACTION STEP

Log in to your ScoreApp portal and edit your results page. Enable the dynamic content in your overall score and create some unique text for each of your scoring tiers. Let people know what it means to score low, medium or high and give people a customised next step based on their score. Once you have the hang of it, you can use dynamic content in the category scores and the call-to-action sections.

A DYNAMIC PDF REPORT

An advanced feature in ScoreApp is the PDF report generator. This allows you to create a special report that people receive via email. The report automatically has their name and the date they took the scorecard on the cover. It contains their scores and you can edit the amount of content you'd like to appear based on the scoring tiers.

You can easily change the colours, fonts and images on the report to match your branding and your personal style. The PDF is an impressive experience for the people who receive it and typically your customers will save it and even print it out.

Our 'Key Person of Influence Scorecard' automatically generates a PDF report. As we have mentioned, it is common for people to bring a printed version to a sales meeting with their notes written on it ready to discuss.

It's not essential for all scorecards to have a PDF version but it works particularly well for professional services and businesses that intend on showing their client how much they have improved in a tangible way by comparing two reports taken at different times.

67% of consumers believe brands should automatically adjust their content according to the current context for a satisfactory personalised experience.[13]

ACTION STEP

Ask your clients if they would value a report showing them insights and making recommendations about their situation. Ask them if they would like to complete this report several times a year to track their progress. If you get the thumbs-up from your top clients, you might want to set up this feature for them and let ScoreApp deliver this experience.

NEXT STEPS

Once someone has seen their results and are clear about where they can improve if they want to, they want to know what to do next. Don't leave people guessing; give them specific instructions or a clear offer.

You can use dynamic content for this step too and present people with a special offer that's right for them, based on the scoring tiers. You might decide that you want to give low scorers a ticket to an appropriate event, send intermediate scorers a book for free and arrange a one-to-one call, and present high scorers with an offer to join a special mastermind session that is only for people at their level.

Perfect next steps to recommend after someone takes your scorecard are:

» **Sales meeting/discovery session** – If you know someone is a suitable client, book them in to talk to you as soon as you can. You can give people a link straight to your diary to book themselves into a one-to-one meeting to discuss their scorecard results and what they can do to improve (we use Calendly for this and it works nicely).

» **Introduction/strategy workshop** – If you are comfortable presenting to groups of people, you can host a regular workshop. This could be a live event, in a boardroom or an online webinar (we use Zoom.us).

» **Relevant content** – If you know people need some more warming up before they buy, you could recommend the right content for them to consume next. It's easy to give people videos, podcast episodes, reports or books as a way to engage further.

» **Product recommendation** – Some people who have taken a scorecard are ready to buy the solution then and there. If your scorecard is crafted well enough, a perfectly selected product offer could be the most obvious next step. If it seems like the offer is generic and gets recommended to everyone regardless of how they answered the questions, it will probably not be welcomed.

ACTION STEP

Set up a CTA on your results page. You could invite people to book into an event, watch a video or book a call to discuss their results. If you make a product offer, be sure it appears relevant by basing it on how they answered the questions.

PRO TIP

Record a few variations of a video that is focused on each of the tiers. Set up the dynamic content to show the right video to people based on their scores – it feels like you are talking directly to them and quickly builds your relationship.

THE DATA

When someone completes their scorecard, they see their results and the dynamic content, and in your ScoreApp portal, you will see all of the data that was collected.

It is a magical experience the first time you click into your portal and see warm leads appear. With each lead appear dozens of useful facts. You'll see the information they provided about themselves when they started the scorecard and filled in the lead form – typically their name, email and location. The ScoreApp system will automatically search the internet for a photo of the person and guess their nearest city location.

The next thing you'll see is a summary of how they scored. You'll have their overall score and their category scores. When you look closer, you'll also be able to see exactly how they answered each question. Sometimes, knowing how someone answered a few key questions can completely change the way you follow up with them. For example, if someone answered 'yes' to the question 'Are you currently looking for a supplier to work with?', you would want to get on the phone to them as soon as possible.

> **59% of consumers find that personalised engagement based on past interactions is important to winning their custom.[14]**

Once you are collecting data in ScoreApp, you'll also be able to see overall statistics about how people answer your questions. It can be a real eye-opener to find out that only a small percentage of your market answers 'yes' to a certain question. This aggregate data is powerful for generating new product ideas and marketing messages, or to write blogs/posts about.

ScoreApp will also help you to improve your scorecard by showing you how your questions are performing; for example, it will highlight any questions that people frequently abandon or take a long time to answer. When you spot questions that slow people down, consider editing them to make them easier or less confrontational.

ACTION STEP

Complete your own scorecard and then look at your data in the portal.

PRO TIP

You can easily export your data or automatically integrate ScoreApp with the most popular CRM systems, such as ActiveCampaign, HubSpot or Salesforce. If you look at the 'integrations' settings, you will see a full list of CRM systems that are supported and you'll be able to have all of your data automatically added to your existing system.

CINDERELLA CLIENTS

We all know Cinderella's story from her point of view, but have you considered it from Prince Charming's perspective? The prince is looking for a wife, he runs a huge event and discovers exactly what he's looking for. Then she disappears. He uses a rigid assessment tool to evaluate thousands of potential Cinderellas before finding her again.

The glass slipper in the story was an exact criterion that allowed the prince to find his true love among thousands of prospects. Your scorecard can be set up so that some of the questions clearly identify the clients that are a perfect match for what you do.

Until now, it has been almost impossible to easily find these Cinderella clients at scale. It is beyond most businesses to gather thousands of potential clients and then somehow analyse them all to identify the one they're looking for. ScoreApp makes this process quick and easy.

If you add questions that identify specific types of people, you can create special offers just for them. ScoreApp has an advanced feature called 'Audiences' which gives you the power to create a narrow criterion for potential clients from your questions and only show those people a special offer.

To see your premium offer, a person might have to answer in the affirmative to three or four questions indicating they have a budget and a problem they need solving that you can address. When they see the specific offer perfectly fitting their needs, it's a magical happily-ever-after moment.

'I love it! ScoreApp gives our team such powerful insights about what to do with a lead. We get hundreds of leads per week and it really helps us to segment our database in a way that we clearly know who to spend more time with.'

— Allan Dib, author of *The 1-Page Marketing Plan*

PRO TIP

Think about your best example of a perfect client. Make a list of two to four questions you could ask to identify whether they fit the description you have in mind, then consider what you would say to them or offer them once you knew they were a perfect client. Make that a special offer on the results page of your scorecard for audiences who answer qualifying questions.

CASE STUDY: ROBOT MASCOT

Robot Mascot helps founders and entrepreneurs raise capital by creating a winning-pitch formula that captivates investors. Within eighteen months, Robot Mascot has gone from a relatively unknown player in the investment space to the UK's leading pitch agency and they are crediting their 500% year-on-year growth to ScoreApp.

THE CHALLENGE

Prior to discovering ScoreApp in the summer of 2020, Robot Mascot focused their marketing efforts on building credibility and trust through in-person networking events and by leveraging their company's blog. Because of their proactive approach, they were having lots of fantastic conversations but few of these were converting into leads for their business.

Their problem was that people didn't understand how to work with them and, unable to self-diagnose their pitch shortcoming, Robot Mascot struggled to communicate their value, resulting in missed opportunities.

THE SOLUTION

James and his team launched the 'Pitch Ready Scorecard' that assesses founders and entrepreneurs on their ability to pitch for assessment. Three key areas –

business plan, projections and pitching skills – form their scorecard categories.

By harnessing the dynamic content functionality on their results page, they can create the right messaging depending on each person's final score. For their ideal clients, they have a clear call to action (CTA) where they can speak to someone quickly and effectively.

They keep less suitable clients in their ecosystem by offering a copy of their book, free helpful resources and links to stay connected through social media.

In either case, each person has a more personal and customised experience based on their answers.

PROMOTION

Almost every Robot Mascot CTA is now 'Take the Scorecard'.

This includes in Facebook and Google ads, on their website banner, in blog posts and social media, in their webinar strategy and even in co-founder James's best-selling book, *Investable Entrepreneur*.[15]

Due to the increase in leads, the team decided to create a second scorecard called the 'Eligibility Assessment' that would act as a qualifier when booking in an intro-ductory call.

This scorecard has saved them time by making sure that they are only speaking to highly qualified people who are the right fit for their services or who are at the right stage of the buying process.

THE RESULTS

Within the first twelve months, they had increased their revenue by 300% with the scorecard as the main CTA and lead generator. Eighteen months later, this is now closer to 500%.

They generate 180 leads per month (roughly forty-five leads per week) with a sales call conversion rate of 50%.

The scorecard has an 80% completion rate and they are closing one in every two sales conversations – all while spending less than 10% of revenue on marketing.

STEP 4: MARKETING AND SALES

Now that you have a scorecard set up and ready to go, you can turn on the tap and get warm, qualified leads flowing in to make more sales.

Use the data to improve your products, services and marketing messages, which all lead to better clients, higher prices, more people buying from you, growth, profitability and more fun.

PROMOTING YOUR SCORECARD

In the first week of your scorecard being live, promote it gently to get a few people taking it so you can capture their feedback.

Put a post on one of your social media profiles, along the lines of:

'I've noticed that a lot of people struggle to achieve <result that your customers want>, even after they've tried <typical action one> or <typical action two>. I'm launching a scorecard to help people identify the best ways they can get the results they want even if they are <typical emotional resistance>. It's pretty simple: you answer some questions and automatically receive customised recommendations. I've only just set it up, so I'd really love some feedback please. Here's the link...'

The goal is to get feedback on how to improve your scorecard, so try to talk to people straight after they've completed it and ask them:

» Was the landing page clear, credible and enticing? Is there anything you think I should change about it?

» Was the questionnaire engaging and easy to answer? Did it seem like there were too many or too few questions? Is there anything I could improve?

» Was the results page valuable? Did you feel it spoke directly to you and gave you clear next steps? Is there anything you feel I should do differently?

With this feedback from a few typical clients, you can make some final adjustments before promoting your scorecard more actively.

There are eight highly effective ways to promote your scorecard:

1. **Website banner** – On your existing website, put a special banner or a pop-up that takes people to your scorecard landing page. One of our clients started getting between six and eight leads per day when they added a scorecard banner. Prior to that, their site had anonymous traffic which wasn't much good to them.

2. **Email signature** – You probably send hundreds of emails each month. Add an automatic signature to your emails that tells people to take your scorecard. Mine says, 'Take the Key Person of Influence Scorecard and improve your ability to influence.'

3. **Email marketing/direct messages** – Most businesses have a sizeable database of existing contacts on their CRM or a reasonable following on their social media profiles. Send a message announcing that your scorecard is live and what it helps people to achieve. It's a powerful way to own and enrich your own unique database.

4. **Social media profiles and posts** – You can post about your scorecard on all of your social media profiles. As something new you have done, people are happy to learn more about it. At a later date, you can post about the statistics you gather from your scorecard data. It's also easy to add your scorecard link to your social media profile contact information.

5. **Podcasts/videos/blogs/books** – The scorecard is the perfect next step for someone who enjoys your media content. If someone has just watched your YouTube video, get them to complete a scorecard as a next step – they go from an anonymous viewer to a warm, qualified lead on your database. Some of the hottest leads you will ever get are people who have engaged with a

few pieces of your online content first and then completed a scorecard.

6.   **Events/workshops** – A scorecard can be used before, during or after an event. Before the event, people can complete a scorecard to get their ticket or they can do a scorecard in the time between booking and attending. During a workshop, you can instruct participants to complete a scorecard as an activity in the programme. Afterwards, you can reconnect with attendees and discover the impact of the event using a scorecard. Most organisers know very little about the people who attend their events; scorecards turn that around.

7.   **Advertising** – I am a massive fan of advertising but it takes time and money to make it work. It's vital to calculate an allowable cost per sale and an allowable cost per lead when running ads; then keep adapting until you can reliably achieve the targets. Facebook and Google ads take time and expertise to keep performing and it can be money well spent to get a professional to set you up. I most often see ScoreApp clients getting a steady stream of leads for $5–$20 per completed scorecard – if that's feasible, it could be the key to scaling your business.

8. **Joint venture partnerships** – When ads get too expensive or I want to remove my reliance on them, I turn to joint venture partnerships. I look for businesses that are in my marketplace but don't directly compete with what I do. I approach them with a deal to cross-promote each other and to pay a small fee per lead to balance any situation where one business gets more leads than the other. A typical joint venture will involve them emailing their mailing list for me to recommend my scorecard and I will pay £10 per completed scorecard that comes in. In return, I can email my list to them too.

9. **Enrich and segment your existing data** – You probably have an existing list of basic contact information, such as name and email, for thousands of people. Use your scorecard to deepen your knowledge for each contact record you already possess. Once you know more about each person, you can segment your list into categories of people who would be suitable for specific offers and promotions.

'I spent £125 on ads and got sixty-seven qualified leads. I've never had anything like it.'

— Helen Pritchard, coach

ACTION STEP

Download our extended resources kit for launching and promoting your scorecard: www.scoreapp.com/launch-quiz-checklist

---

FOLLOWING UP AND MAKING SALES

Google has armies of salespeople and they are the most automated business on the planet. Rolex has armies of salespeople and they are the most recognised luxury brand. Apple does endless amounts of sales training and it has some of the most recognisable products on Earth.

If the top brands and businesses rely heavily on salespeople making calls, having conversations, following up with leads and handling objections, your business needs to embrace the sales process too.

Having a powerful marketing system like ScoreApp working in your business doesn't mean you can sit back and let the sales take care of themselves – it will give you plenty of opportunities to have quality sales conversations. ScoreApp generates hot, data-rich leads for you, but if you don't do anything with them those people will go and buy from a business that is more active in its sales approach.

If I was in charge of growing your business, I would likely hire more people in a sales role, make sure they were well trained and get them talking to warm leads every day. For most established businesses, I would launch a scorecard to the existing client database or social media following and then talk with everyone who took the scorecard. An influx of new business is probably a lot closer than you think and a scorecard plus a sales meeting might be the only thing needed to unlock it.

Appointment setting

A perfect next step for many businesses is to book someone into a sales meeting or an event/workshop to push things forward. I have built several fast-growth businesses and always hired in-house appointment setters who become reliable at putting the right leads in front of me or my salespeople.

In the days before scorecards, we used to cold call people, but even when they would pick up the phone a lot of them didn't recognise our company brand and ended the call quickly.

A cold call typically starts with the caller dialling someone on a list, identifying themselves, where they are calling from and why they are calling. Most people don't like cold-calling and most people don't like being called out of the blue by someone they don't know. Cold-calling is dead.

Following up with scorecard leads is completely different. You aren't calling people randomly, you're responding to their signal of interest by calling them shortly after they've completed a scorecard. You already know a lot about them and you can reference the information they've given you.

This is a typical call from Sophie, an appointment setter on my team, to Jo, a potential client who has completed a scorecard:

Jo: Hello?

Sophie: Hi, is that Jo?

Jo: Yes, it is.

Sophie: It's Sophie here. You took the 'Key Person of Influence Scorecard' yesterday and I wanted to touch base with you about it. I saw that you scored 54% out of 100% for your overall score. Are you too busy to talk for a minute or two – I'll keep it quick?

Jo: Ah, I'm pretty busy but if it's quick...

Sophie: I need to keep this call short as well but I knew it would be valuable to touch base with you.

I talk to hundreds of entrepreneurs who have taken the 'Key Person of Influence Scorecard', and 54% is actually a good score. You have strong foundations in place, which is the hardest part. The rest is just adding some tactics to get your message out to more people. I see that you are really strong with pitching skills, you scored seven out of ten, but your weakest score was for product creation, which was three out of ten. That means you are confident pitching the value of what you do but you haven't created enough products for people to buy. Is that fair to say?

Jo: Yeah, that's true.

Sophie: As I said, I have to keep this call quick because I have to touch base with a few other entrepreneurs this morning; however, I've looked at how you answered the questions and I would really love to make a time for you to get some additional value from us. In particular, I think we can focus on improving your product score, which would have the biggest impact.

I'd like to send you a physical copy of the book *Key Person of Influence*. Is that OK?

Jo: Yeah, that would be nice of you.

Sophie: If you're open to it, I'd also like to get you a free pass to a workshop we're running this week, specifically about improving the scores in the 'Key Person of Influence Scorecard'. I know your time is valuable so I want to let you know that we've recently won two major awards for the quality of the work we do with entrepreneurs. I think you'll get relevant ideas if you come and join this workshop. Would you like a free ticket?

Jo: Yeah, that sounds good.

Sophie: I thought you might. Let me get your details so I can send you the book and get you a ticket to the workshop.

...Sophie gets details...

Sophie: All done. The book is on the way and the ticket should be in your inbox. Pretty soon I think you will be implementing some of the tactics we recommend for entrepreneurs. Have you got any questions for me at this stage?

Jo: No, that sounds good. I'll look forward to it.

Sophie: Excellent. If you need to get in touch, just reply to the email I sent you. Hope you enjoy the workshop next Tuesday at 2pm. Bye for now.

You'll notice that Sophie referenced the data from the scorecard quickly. She mentioned the overall score straight away. Next, she talked about the highest and lowest category scores. We call this the 'seesaw technique' – it gives people positive vibes for something they are good at then shows them the area they could improve most. Once Jo twigged that the call wasn't cold and that it was focused on an area she wanted to improve, she was happy to talk about next steps. Feel free to adapt this script to suit your business.

'I've always hated sales calls because I feel like I'm asking nosey questions for the first fifteen to thirty minutes. When I talk to people about their scorecard all of that information is already in front of me, I can move straight into making the right proposal much faster.'

— Karen Dwyer, MS to Success

Sales meetings

Now that you've got lots of warm leads, make sure you talk to them and turn them into sales.

Here's a cruel irony: the people who typically buy from you don't truly want to buy from you. If I truly loved fitness, I wouldn't need a fitness trainer. I would jump out of bed each day and go for a run while listening to fitness books. If I truly loved finance, I wouldn't need a chief financial officer. I'd already be confident about my numbers. If I truly loved investing, I wouldn't need a financial planner. I'd already have a great investing plan in motion.

The things we buy are often things we are sitting on the fence about. We want the results but we struggle to know how to get them or to do the work required. We need support or tools to make it happen.

Some of the best clients you will ever have start off feeling hesitant about what you do. They need some convincing, they need to know you care enough to call them, they need to know you are confident they can do it, because they think they aren't.

Many of your best clients have tried things before that didn't work. They bought that foolproof software and it made them into the fool. They spent money on a top supplier and the project didn't complete the way they wanted it to. They bought the package but failed to unwrap it. They're not just sceptical of you, they're sceptical of themselves.

The majority of your big sales will come from a sales process where you or your team talk to people one-to-one. You'll have a conversation that reassures people that what you do will be worth the money and the commitment.

A ScoreApp scorecard doesn't remove the need to talk to people. It gives you more people to talk to. It gives you topics to discuss that matter most. It gives you a way to know who you should talk to first.

Make the scorecard results a central feature in your sales meeting. Ask people what it revealed to them about their situation. Give them your insights on their situation. Clarify their goals and the obstacles they think could stop them getting what they want.

You might want to focus on specific answers to individual questions. You might ask, 'You answered yes to the question "Do you often struggle with XYZ?" Why do you think that is?' These types of questions help you to better understand what your client needs and how to get them rapid results.

The scorecard is a diagnostic tool, so your sales meeting is about resolving the issues that your potential client self-assessed. Making a sale is about providing a sensible solution that resolves the tension they have identified on the scorecard.

'Our whole sales process has changed since using ScoreApp. I actually can't imagine having to go back to our old approach of talking to people without knowing in advance what they need my help with.'

— TJ Power, employee wellness specialist

Repeat what worked

If you go to the well and pull up a bucket full of water, go back to the well and get another.

Some people promote their ScoreApp scorecard in September, get lots of new leads but don't do the same thing in October, November and December. They think that their potential customers are going to say, 'Hey wait a second, you promoted your scorecard last month – you can't do that again!'

The truth is your customers don't remember what you did last month. People need to see things multiple times before they see it the *first* time.

I've run the same ads for years in a row because they keep on working. The same ads to the same audience brought in scorecard leads for £9–£12 per lead – for years. I have repeated emails to my database because they were effective the year before. I have posted similar content on LinkedIn asking

people if they want to get a free report from my scorecard –
and it keeps working the second, third and fourth time.

When I figure out a sales script that works, we use it every
week. When I notice ads that work, we keep running them.
If we sponsor an event and it produces results, we book it
straight in again the following year.

If something is working, don't stop doing it even if your
business can't handle more customers. I've seen ScoreApp
clients launch their scorecard and generate dozens of new
clients – more than they can handle. Rather than starting a
waiting list, they switch off their scorecard and halt promotions.
Predictably, a few months later they have capacity and they
need to start promoting from scratch again.

A better approach would be to leave the campaigns running,
communicate with people that you have a waiting list and
invite people to join it. When an abundance of leads keep
coming in, you end up oversubscribed; you can confidently
increase your prices and cherry-pick the best clients you want
to work with. You can also add new versions of your products
or services that are more scalable and less exclusive.

The best brands in the world – like Ferrari, Rolex and
Apple – always keep promoting themselves even when they
have a waiting list.

If you do something that works, do it again and keep
doing it.

CASE STUDY: TICK THOSE BOXES

Tick Those Boxes works with high-performing coaches, executives and their teams to ensure full accountability and execution in meeting their goals.

In the first thirty days, Tick Those Boxes generated AU$60,000 directly from their scorecard.

THE CHALLENGE

Like any service-based business, finding the right audience, identifying the problem and communicating the value you bring is the holy grail of generating sales. As an accomplished professional, Darren is well respected and visible within his field, but, even with such a great brand reputation, Darren is always looking at ways to improve the sales process.

Darren and his team wanted a more robust system that would consistently generate leads and provide a clear ROI.

THE SOLUTION

Tick Those Boxes launched the 'Accountability Scorecard' to assess coaches and executive teams on how accountable they are when it comes to working towards their goals. The 'Accountability Scorecard' created an online asset for the business that works automatically in the background and is perfect for running ads and personalising their message. It works seamlessly with their website branding, connects to their customer relationship management (CRM) system and automatically filters through into their email nurture campaign.

Focusing on adding value through the results page, Tick Those Boxes then break down scores to provide tailored insights and highlighted areas for improvement. As a bonus for taking the scorecard, they offer 50% off *The Accountability Advantage* book and a free sixty-minute discovery call.

But they don't stop there...

One of the highlights of taking this scorecard is the fully customised, nineteen-page PDF report that is delivered to your inbox on completion. Jam-packed with value that highlights Darren's team as the industry leaders, it provides tangible next steps.

PROMOTION

Tick Those Boxes used a mixed strategy of paid and organic marketing.

They decided to leverage Facebook advertising by spending AU$10 a day on advertising. The advert asked, 'How accountable are you?', as Darren felt that would trigger interest and align with his scorecard's message.

The ads over the first thirty days generated 1,702 visitors to the landing page.

THE RESULTS

Within the first thirty days, seventy-five people had completed the scorecard, with an average completion time of three minutes. Darren and his team received five times the amount of booked discovery calls, and four times the amount of new clients on their AU$15,000 package.

This all amounted to an 80% conversion rate, resulting in AU$60,000 worth of new business.

SCOREAPP'S MORE ADVANCED FEATURES

We've tried to keep things simple and straightforward in this book while you're setting up your first scorecard marketing campaign. As you become familiar with ScoreApp, you can explore some of the more advanced features and customisations. These include:

» **Abandon emails** – ScoreApp can automatically send people an email if they stop the quiz and encourage them to pick up where they left off.

» **Ad tracking** – ScoreApp allows you to use your Facebook or Google tracking pixels to improve your advertising results.

» **Audiences** – You can create special audiences on ScoreApp based on how people answer a question or a combination of questions. Once you have an audience set up, you can show those audiences special offers.

» **Custom domains** – It is easy to make ScoreApp appear to be a part of your existing website using custom domains.

» **Data analysis** – You can look at your data in several useful ways. You can see the questions people abandon or are slow to answer. You can view the aggregate statistics for your questions.

» **Experiments** – This allows you to randomly test two landing pages against each other to see which one is most effective.

» **Integrations** – You can integrate ScoreApp with your preferred CRM system using an application programming interface (API) key or API URL. This allows ScoreApp to send the data it collects to your existing system.

» **Multiple scorecards** – You can have several scorecards running under one account. Each scorecard can have different landing pages, questions and results.

» **PDF reports** – ScoreApp gives you the capability to send people a customised report. This report features dynamic content and is presented in a way that adds value and tangibility to your scorecard.

» **Referral programme** – You will automatically have a referral link in your account. Anyone who joins ScoreApp through your link will receive an extended free trial and you will earn a commission on their subscription fee.

» **Social sharing** – ScoreApp lets you customise the text and the primary image shown when someone shares the link to your scorecard.

» **SEO** – ScoreApp has a number of search engine optimisation features that align to best practices in search engine optimisation. For example, you can add alternative text to your images.

Note: Some of these features are only available on the advanced subscription options.

A NEW ASSET FOR YOUR BUSINESS

A successful scorecard marketing campaign is simple. You need a compelling landing page, a questionnaire, personalised results and a sensible approach to promotions and sales. After completing these four steps, you will have created a valuable new asset for your business.

In business, an asset is anything that continues to add value when you are away on holiday. In this case, your scorecard would continue to function. It would be a point of contact for your future clients, collecting valuable data and providing your salespeople with leads.

All of the data you collect is also an asset. In the short term, you have hot leads to talk to and you know a lot about each person so you make better sales conversions. In the medium term, you have valuable insights about all of your customers and you can improve your products or your marketing based on what you learn. Long-term, you have a database available to launch new products.

All stress in business is typically an 'asset deficiency'. Without marketing assets, it's impossible to get reliable marketing results. If you have the right assets in place, they do the heavy lifting and the stress goes away.

Giving your people the right assets makes their job much easier and they become happier and more effective. Imagine a salesperson thrown into a role without training, without sales materials and without warm leads to speak with; they quickly get rejected and start blaming themselves or their boss for their poor performance.

If that same person had the right assets, they would be more likely to succeed. If they had training and sales materials and were talking to hot leads, they would convert those leads into paying customers, making everyone happy. It wasn't the salesperson that was the problem. It was the assets they had to leverage that made the difference. Your business is an ecosystem of assets being leveraged by you and your people. The better your assets, the more fun you have and the more money you make.

Imagine if you wanted to sell your business and you told the potential acquirer, 'We have 10,000 people on our database and we know fifty things about each of them!' That would be a seriously impressive reason for them to buy your business instead of another, especially if the business had a scorecard in place that continued to bring in more warm leads every week. They would see your scorecard as a scalable and repeatable system for making sales.

The scorecard is a marketing and sales asset. It builds a database asset; it is a product-for-prospects asset plus a channel-to-market asset. Your scorecard is powerful because it is doing many jobs for your business, making your business more scalable, more enjoyable and more profitable.

DON'T LET ANYTHING STAND IN YOUR WAY

At ScoreApp, we get a notification whenever someone cancels their subscription or chooses not to go beyond their free trial period. We can see the main reasons why people leave.

50% of the people who leave say they didn't have enough time to set it up

Automation does require an initial investment of time and creativity, but it rapidly pays you back. A few hours spent setting up a scorecard on ScoreApp speeds up every sale and shaves time from every sales conversation you have. Building a business that runs smoothly with minimal effort from you and your people requires some sophisticated systems to be running in the background. Our team have invested thousands of hours into perfecting this system and all it needs you to do is block out a couple of hours to make it part of your business. Don't be the 'busy fool' who doesn't have the time to grab a bicycle because he's too busy running around on foot.

ACTION STEP

Block out an hour or two in the diary and get it set up. If you get stuck, use the help button in your portal which is always at the bottom-right of the screen. A real person will get in touch with you to offer support.

If you prefer, you can get our ScoreApp enterprise team to build a custom scorecard for you (for an additional cost).

11% of people say they couldn't come up with questions or categories

It takes creativity to come up with a questionnaire and many people are hard on themselves because they don't get it right the first time. The people who succeed with ScoreApp often use our templates at first and make a few edits. As they get more comfortable, they make the scorecard unique to their business. Thanks to our expert team, everything is ready to go so you can get started with minimal fuss, launching a scorecard the easy way and then fine-tuning it over time.

ACTION STEP

Come along to one of our 'Setup and Score' workshops where we answer questions and give suggestions live on Zoom. You can also join our Facebook group (www.facebook.com/groups/scoreapp) and get suggestions from other ScoreApp clients.

24% of people said they got set up but didn't get enough leads

A scorecard is a marketing asset and it needs you to consistently promote it so that people discover its value. The bigger your audience, the greater the number of people who will take your scorecard each month. Even with a small audience, a scorecard is the key to getting the most from the people who are engaging and gaining valuable insights that will resonate with more people. Persist with your marketing efforts and accept feedback from customers and mentors to improve your conversions. It's a process not a destination.

ACTION STEP

Use our guide '29 Ways to Launch Your Scorecard' so that you have plenty of approaches to try (www.scoreapp. com/launch-quiz-checklist). Go back over them regularly and double down on what works.

9% of people who left said the functionality they wanted was missing

When we explored this more deeply, we often found that people wanted the scorecard to demonstrate more complex decision-making capability. This relies on things like 'decision trees' and 'branching logic'. Some people wanted survey tools, calculators or the option for people to sit an exam. We're focused on the outcome of generating warm, qualified leads for businesses that typically need to build a relationship before making a sale, so we deliberately stop ourselves from creating features that don't line up specifically with that goal. We think the fastest way to make ScoreApp less powerful is to add dozens of features that overcomplicate the job our clients are trying to do. We've tested complex scorecards against more simple ones and simple always wins when it comes to generating warm leads.

ACTION STEP

Use ScoreApp for lead generation and find other tools that are specifically developed for exams, surveys, calculators or complex diagnosis. If you want hot leads and to make more sales, our expert team have got your back.

3% of people say they got leads but were not able to convert them

A scorecard is the first step your customers make towards buying from your business but it's not the only step. Customers are spoilt for choice and they often want a lot from you before buying.

It's not uncommon for customers to read something, watch something, take a scorecard, have a meeting, take some time to review a proposal, have another meeting and then buy. It's also important that you keep your sales skills sharp so you can turn interest into action.

ACTION STEP

Do some regular sales role play with your team or with a friend. Use the scorecard as a discussion piece that focuses the conversation on achieving a goal or solving a problem.

SCOREAPP REFERRAL PROGRAMME

Many of our ScoreApp clients get paid each month to have ScoreApp. When you create a ScoreApp account, we automatically give you a referral link so that you can recommend ScoreApp and get a commission. If you love the value ScoreApp brings to your business and you want to share it, send people your link and they can get an extended free trial. If they go ahead and subscribe, you will earn the money we would have otherwise spent on ads (we would rather give you money than Google and Facebook). You can find your referral link and commission report in your account information when you are logged in to ScoreApp.

SET UP AND SCORE!

The United States presidential elections are the most contested, high-stakes marketing campaigns on Earth. As marketing professionals, it's worth tuning out from the politics and paying close attention to the tools, technologies and channels the winning candidate uses to get their message across to voters.

In the 1930s Franklin D Roosevelt (FDR) campaigned for president on the radio. He created something known as the 'fireside chat' to speak directly to voters on a regular basis about the issues that mattered to them as they happened in real time. This technique was revolutionary at the time; it leveraged a national network of radio stations that carried Roosevelt's voice to all corners of the US.

Prior to this, presidents relied on newspaper networks to report on what they had said. Often their words were distorted by journalists and in many cases the tone of voice was lost and the message misread. National radio solved this problem and FDR was the first president to harness the power of radio. In the following decade, radio became the marketing channel of choice for big brands and the key to success was the radio jingle.

In 1960 John F Kennedy (JFK) went head-to-head with Richard Nixon in a live televised debate. Nixon wasn't comfortable under the hot studio lights and he continuously wiped his brow and lips with a handkerchief. On radio, a move like this would have gone unnoticed but on TV Nixon looked nervous or stressed out. By contrast, JFK seemed relaxed and poised; he had been on TV a lot more and was prepared for the studio environment. People who listened to the debate on radio thought that Nixon had won but the majority of the population had watched it on TV and voted for the candidate who performed for the screen.

In the decade that followed, TV became the number one medium for reaching consumers. Brands moved their budgets from radio to television. The key to successful marketing was to become proficient in the thirty-second commercial.

In 2008 Barack Obama was the first presidential candidate to use social media as a way to engage with voters. His campaign managers were early employees of Facebook and they encouraged him to embrace the online platforms. His website featured a section called 'Obama Everywhere' which aligned with his Twitter, Facebook, YouTube and other social media accounts. He uploaded more, he shared more and he responded more than all of the other candidates – and he won more votes as a result.

The following decade, social media marketing became the main arena for brands to reach their customers. Every big brand moved their spend towards the same platforms

Obama had used to win the election. Big brands hired social media marketers, and agencies moved their focus onto content creation to feed the endless need for social feeds.

In 2016 Donald Trump shocked the world with his win against the political establishment. He had engaged data analytics companies to create a marketing campaign unlike anything the world had seen before. His marketing team was able to get vast amounts of data about voters and then deliver uniquely targeted campaigns to each voter based on their existing views.

He focused all his money on the locations that mattered most based on the data and the likelihood of winning the most electoral college votes, not the popular vote. Data informed every decision about what to say to the people that would deliver him the White House.

Regardless of your political persuasions, there's a clear lesson from the Trump 2016 campaign that data analytics is a powerful tool in marketing. Big brands are now adopting the approach of gathering as much data about people as they can and then hyper-targeting their marketing messages to people based on their existing preferences. Eventually, every marketing campaign will speak directly to the person who's seeing it.

DATA IS THE LIFEBLOOD OF MARKETING

In the late 2000s I was giving talks to entrepreneurs, advising them to 'become a media business'. I said that whatever business they thought they were in, they were also in the media business. It was pretty radical at the time but today it has become a widely understood idea. Most hair salons have active Instagram accounts with photos and videos uploaded multiple times per day. Business coaches host their own podcasts and video channels. Lawyers and accountants are actively blogging on LinkedIn. None of that seemed likely prior to 2010.

Today I tell people to 'become a data business'. Whatever business you think you are in, you are also a data analytics business. The world is becoming too noisy for generic media content to make an impact – too many people are pumping out too much content. Customers want things to be personal to them, and that requires data.

In the 2010s the more content you produced the more sales you would make. That's coming to an end now, as people are drowning in an endless stream of amazing but generic content.

The more data you collect now, the more sales you will make in the future. Data is the key to cutting through the noise and connecting with people.

Personalised marketing presents a completely new landscape where neighbours who live side by side on the same street might see and hear completely different information about the world. Before this era of data-driven marketing, advertising and campaigning were conducted out in the open for everyone to see and evaluate the same information. Going forward, every person is living within their own news and information bubble that is being constructed just for them.

90% of US consumers find marketing personalisation appealing.[16]

The ultimate goal of marketing is to create marketing campaigns for one. Each individual sees things that are uniquely relevant to them.

A single mother, working in retail, who enjoys CrossFit classes and has concerns about the school curriculum will see information that perfectly aligns to her world. Her elderly neighbour in the flat below, who is concerned with healthcare budgets, loves crime novels and is planning a trip to Tuscany, will have a completely different experience of the online world.

All personal data is up for grabs to inform the marketing machines. The locations you visit, your sexual and political preferences, your hobbies, your search results, your friends' preferences, the videos you watch and countless other things all give advertisers more clues on how to approach you.

As we move into a world powered by Artificial Intelligence (AI), this will only get more detailed. If you wear a smartwatch, AI algorithms can determine what you're doing from the movement of your hands. Based on the tone of your voice, AI can know who you're talking to and how you feel about them. If an AI can see video footage of your face, it can spot micro-expressions that reveal your thoughts and emotions on a topic.

It seems a little dystopian to many people but consumer trends indicate strongly that people want personalisation and they are willing to give up information about themselves to get it. In the same way that social media seemed foreign and complicated at first, data analytics will move from the shadows and become commonplace in every successful small business.

64% of consumers agree with businesses saving their purchase history and preferences in order to provide personalised experiences.[17]

You want to be an early adopter with this trend. While everyone is still furiously producing content for Instagram, Twitter and YouTube, you can make the shift towards collecting and using data to deliver personalisation. You can leapfrog out of the saturated social media landscape and into the flourishing data analytics world.

Small businesses need to adapt fast to this way of marketing. Being personalised to people's needs was once the domain of boutique, local small businesses but it is now the strength of big brands like Amazon, Spotify and Facebook. Small businesses need to discover ways to collect more (much, much more) data about their customers and then use it to create laser-focused marketing campaigns to individuals based on that data.

Collecting name and email is no longer enough. Your business must conduct surveys, scorecards and quizzes to have access to unique data insights. Proprietary data enables you to deliver a message that lands.

The more data you collect, the less you need to spend on sales and marketing. The more data you make, the easier it is to make sales and to charge what you're worth.

Data allows you to customise and target your message to the right people in the right place at the right time. In the future, companies that waste their marketing budgets on people who aren't interested in the message at that moment will be put out of business by companies that are using data to communicate more powerfully.

CONCLUSION

I've shown how a scorecard helps to diagnose a problem and/ or highlight strengths and weaknesses. It offers immediate value with dynamic recommendations. It's available online 24/7 and takes just a few minutes to complete.

ScoreApp is the software that makes it easy to run scorecard marketing campaigns. It's exactly what I wished I had when I found huge success using this type of marketing in the 2010s. If your business needs to talk to someone and qualify that person's situation before you can properly sell to them, a ScoreApp scorecard is a game changer. If your business would benefit from having a steady stream of qualified leads to talk to, this marketing system will be a big part of your future success.

Why is your best friend your best friend? It's because they know a lot about you. You can connect and laugh together so easily because you have common language and shared experiences. You can pick up on conversations you had from years ago and discuss memories you both understand.

All of this is based on data. Not data in the way we normally think about it – but in a way we should be thinking about it. Data collection, insights and utilisation sound pretty clinical but they are the key to creating deep affection towards your brand.

When you think about data, think about connection, understanding, empathy and passion. Let data be a tool for tuning into people and getting a view of their reality. If you think it's about spreadsheets, facts, figures and statistics you've missed the point.

If you get it right, people won't just buy from you, they will absolutely love your business and your brand and the impact you have in their world.

I'm looking forward to seeing your scorecard marketing campaign up and running, hearing about how many quality leads came in and how many new sales your business made.

RESOURCES

Get a free extended trial for ScoreApp.com:
   www.scoreapp.com/booktrial-offer

Join the ScoreApp Facebook community:
   www.facebook.com/groups/scoreapp

Check out our tutorials and workshops on YouTube:
   www.youtube.com/c/ScoreApp

Access our launch and promotion resources:
   www.scoreapp.com/launch-quiz-checklist

Learn from our strategies for converting leads into
appointments and sales:
   www.scoreapp.com/convert-quiz-leads-sales

REFERENCES

1   Accenture Interactive (2018) 'Making It Personal: Why brands must move from communication to conversation for greater personalization', www.accenture.com/_acnmedia/PDF-77/Accenture-Pulse-Survey.pdf, accessed 31 May 2022

2   Salesforce (2022) 'What are customer expectations, and how have they changed?', www.salesforce.com/resources/articles/customer-expectations, accessed 31 May 2022

3   Think with Google (no date) 'Zero Moment of Truth', www.thinkwithgoogle.com/marketing-strategies/micro-moments/zero-moment-truth, accessed 31 May 2022

4   R Dunbar *How Many Friends Does One Person Need?* (Faber, 2011)

5   Wunderkind (2022) 'The SmarterHQ offering is now Wunderkind audiences', www.wunderkind.co/blog/article/smarterhq-wunderkind-audiences, accessed 31 May 2022

6   Accenture Interactive (2018) 'Making It Personal: Why brands must move from communication to conversation for greater personalization', www.accenture.com/_acnmedia/PDF-77/Accenture-Pulse-Survey.pdf, accessed 31 May 2022

7   Salesforce (2022) 'What are customer expectations, and how have they changed?', www.salesforce.com/resources/articles/customer-expectations, accessed 31 May 2022

8   Salesforce (2022) 'Meet Marketing Cloud Personalization powered by Interaction Studio', www.salesforce.com/products/marketing-cloud/customer-interaction, accessed 31 May 2022

9   Segment (2017) 'The 2017 State of Personalization Report', http://grow.segment.com/Segment-2017-Personalization-Report.pdf, accessed 31 May 2022

10 SR Covey, *The 7 Habits of Highly Effective People* (Free Press, 2004)

11 R Kiyosaki, *Rich Dad's Cashflow Quadrant: Rich dad's guide to financial freedom* (Business Plus, 2012)

12 J Vocell (2018) 'Personalized calls to action perform 202% better than basic CTAs', HubSpot, https://blog.hubspot.com/marketing/personalized-calls-to-action-convert-better-data, accessed 31 May 2022

13 CMO by Adobe (2022) https://blog.adobe.com/en/topics/cmo-by-adobe, accessed 31 May 2022

14 Salesforce (2022) 'What are customer expectations, and how have they changed?', www.salesforce.com/resources/articles/customer-expectations, accessed 31 May 2022

15 J Church, *Investable Entrepreneur: How to convince investors your business is the one to back* (Rethink Press, 2020)

16 A Guttman (2021) 'Marketing personalization – statistics and facts', Statista, www.statista.com/topics/4481/personalized-marketing, accessed 31 May 2022

17 S Ghosh (2018) 'Unified Commerce Is Here: The Customer Experience Is Here', Martech Series, https://martechseries.com/analytics/behavioral-marketing/unified-commerce-customer-experience-future

ACKNOWLEDGEMENTS

A special thanks and acknowledgement to the team at ScoreApp, who all relish every single success story we see from our clients.

Steven Oddy is the technological genius behind the development of ScoreApp. Without Steven, all of the ideas in this book would be nothing more than marketing philosophies that would be too hard for most businesses to implement. Steven and his team of developers have taken something as complex as data analytics and made it simple, powerful and fun for businesses of all sizes. They've painstakingly found ways to make the platform easy to use while maintaining the strengths that arise from a complex approach to marketing.

In February 2022, war broke out in Ukraine and our technology development team found their lives tipped upside down. These young men and women who were living normal modern lives and enjoying simple pleasures suddenly had their families ripped apart and their daily reality shattered.

Despite it all, they've remained focused and positive about their work and we've remained committed and supportive of them. Our little team at ScoreApp continues to create and innovate together, and we even still laugh together. We want to acknowledge the unbreakable spirit and resilience shown by our workmates in Ukraine.

OTHER BOOKS BY DANIEL PRIESTLEY

The entrepreneur's journey is predictable. These books guide you through the steps to success.

Entrepreneur Revolution
The world is changing and so must you. Talented people are leaving traditional ways of working behind to start and grow small global businesses. The ideas and strategies that worked in the industrial age are not right for today. This book explores the mindset of successful entrepreneurs and the strategies they use to rapidly launch a business that works.

Key Person of Influence
Every industry revolves around Key People of Influence. Their names come up in conversation, they attract opportunities, they make more money and have more fun. Becoming a Key Person of Influence in your industry is not about the time you've spent working or the academic qualifications you have. As you will see in this book, there are steps you can take to make it into the inner circle of your industry – fast.

Oversubscribed
There are businesses that people line up for. There are brands that have a waiting list of customers who are almost fighting for the opportunity to buy. In a world of endless choices this shouldn't happen but we see it all the time. Restaurants where

you can't get a table. Consultants who are booked up months in advance. Products that sell out on the day they launch. This book explores the strategies that deliberately orchestrate the phenomenon of being oversubscribed.

24 Assets

Income follows assets. Scale follows assets. Fun follows assets. An asset is anything that adds value or solves a problem when you aren't there. Assets do the heavy lifting and make your team more effective at getting results. The most successful businesses now develop digital assets for achieving scale and profit with less stress. This book explores the most powerful digital assets you can develop for your business.

These books by Daniel Priestley are available on Amazon and Audible.

THE AUTHORS

Daniel founded his first company in 2002 in Australia at the age of twenty-one. Before he was twenty-five, he and his business partner Glen Carlson had grown a national business turning over several million dollars.

In 2006 Daniel and Glen moved from Australia to launch a new venture in London. Arriving with only a suitcase and a credit card, Daniel set up a new venture and grew it to seven-figure revenues in under two years. In the process, he became a leading figure in his industry and had the opportunity to be mentored personally by some of the world's top entrepreneurs and leaders.

Daniel and Glen's entrepreneurial career has included starting, building, buying, financing and selling businesses. Daniel and Glen are regarded as among the world's top professional speakers on business and entrepreneurship and regularly speak to large audiences about the entrepreneur journey. Today, Daniel and Glen work to develop entrepreneurs who stand out, scale up and make a positive impact through business. Their Accelerator programme reinvents traditional businesses using a unique approach to personal branding and technology. ScoreApp gives people a powerful tool to find the right clients. Both Glen and Daniel are active in fundraising and supporting charities.

🐦 @danielpriestley, @glencarlson
📷 @danielpriestley, @glencarlson